THE UNDERDOG MANIFESTO

By Gilbert Joa

THE UNDERDOG MANIFESTO

Unleash Your Inner Greatness Even if You Had A Bad Start

Gilbert Joa

The Underdog Manifesto

by Gilbert Joa

1st Edition

The Underdog Manifesto @2020

Gilbert Joa

www.gilbertjoa.com

Introduction

What's an underdog got to do with greatness?

Who is an underdog?

By the Webster dictionary definition, an underdog is "a competitor thought to have little chance of winning a fight or contest" or "a person who has little status in society."

Underdogs hold a special meaning in our hearts. We read about stories of David and Goliaths; we watch movies of underdogs overcoming their situation and rising out stronger than ever. We admire their courage, grit, and perseverance.

If you have ever felt the odds stacked against you, this book is for you. Feeling stuck is something we might feel at one point in our lives or another.

Within these pages, I will also peel back the layers of my life so far. I'll show you how my interpretation of past events and belief patterns held me back for years. I'll share how I used my shortcomings and turned them into an unfair advantage, to build a life that I desire.

I am by no means a so-called "self-made" success guru, nor do I claim myself to be one. Some people had a much harsher reality than I've had. My story will, however, highlight elements of struggles and tribulations that will resonate with you, the reader.

I believe we are all on a life-long journey, and process to uncover and live our most profound truth.

It's like an onion. We are constantly peeling back layers with each new realization we have about ourselves. When we feel like we have done all the work, there's another layer underneath waiting to be discovered. Writing this book, to me, is like peeling my onion. It has been one of the mediums I've used to reach closer to the core. Without further adieu, here is my story.

Chapter 1:
My Story

There are millions around the world living with poor access to water, shelter, and security.

I am lucky not to be in that camp.

Although if I were, it would probably make my story harder to relate to. However, I grew up in a place most are familiar with. A place called 'the middle class'.

While there is nothing wrong with what social-economic standing you are part of, there is a word that sums it up.

That word is 'average.'

Your food and shelter needs are more or less taken care of. You had a decent education, likely a university graduate, and some made it to grad school. If you are in the workforce, you have a stable job that pays modestly. Enough for one major vacation per year in the two weeks work leave you're given.

You can afford to live within your means, without any lavish expenses. The idea of 'living on your terms, or living however you like, is no more than a pipe dream — just wishful thinking.

As a Chinese American, I was born in one of the three Chinatowns in New York City, in the humble neighborhood of Flushing, Queens.

My father was a farmer from rural China living in a small village from Guangdong Province. He left his family at 12 in search of a better life. His first stop was in the Dominican Republic in the 60s, where he stayed with his grandfather and worked at the local restaurant as a waiter.

After spending years in a country torn with civil war, at 19 years old, he made his way to America without a pair of shoes or a dollar to his name. He spent his first night sleeping on a park bench across the street from barely lit sidewalks and a Dunkin Donuts.

My mother, a native of Hong Kong, met my father while he was on a business trip. They were shortly married after, where she then immigrated to America, later giving birth to me.

Even that didn't come easy. My mother had two miscarriages before finally having me on a faithful Saturday.

Living as an Asian in America has its own set of challenges. Income was never stable for our family. My father was a businessman, while my mom stayed at home to take care of my younger brother, sister, and I.

At one point during my childhood, the family fell into hard times. We owed the bank thousands, we had to apply for food stamps, and I wore hand-me-down clothes.

I remember one day I came to school with a T-shirt with sleeves up to my shoulders and shorts that showed my underwear when I sat down.

My classmates teased me non-stop and told me that I dressed like a girl. As one of the few Asian kids in my school, bullying became a commonplace until high school. Racial discrimination and prejudice were a daily occurrence.

I remember telling myself that I wished I wasn't born Asian. *I faced an identity crisis and felt a lost sense of belonging, which played a massive role in my childhood.*

Things weren't any better when it came to my studies. People assumed I was good at math and didn't speak good English. For the most part, I fit into that stereotype.

I struggled with pronouncing and spelling words, and would later realize that I had a degree of dyslexia that made reading comprehension and writing difficult.

Although I was born and raised in the U.S., English was my second language. I was sent to English as a Second Language (ESL) classes because my teachers thought my English was not sufficient enough to be in regular classes.

ESL classes were essentially slower curriculum courses for students who spoke English as a native language. The class was typically comprised of students who were born overseas and immigrated to the U.S.

That experience dealt a massive blow to my confidence. I would later get dismal scores on the reading and writing sections of the SAT, standardized admissions test for universities in the U.S.

I grew up thinking I was terrible at English. This belief held me back from really learning the language. To this day, I have trouble spelling simple words. Auto-correct has been my savior.

My parents expected that I perform well in my studies.

Failing to do so will often be met with harsh criticism, usually starting with these three words, *"Why didn't you......?"*

It was the start of the mental conditioning that would impact my life for many years to come.

I later attended Brooklyn Technical High School in New York City, a specialized school that required an entrance exam. It was the top 3 specialized schools at the time, and you would think I would be thrilled to be accepted.

However, I wasn't. I reprimanded myself for failing to get into the #1 school. I couldn't grasp the idea that most people went to regular schools and that only a small group of students like myself would end up in an elite school.

I developed a sense of entitlement. I felt that I should deserve the best, even though I had never put in the work required to achieve that goal.

My father came to America without a high school degree and managed to graduate with a college degree, half a year early. He did all that while working two jobs on the side to pay himself through college.

As for myself, I took a perfectly good opportunity in high school and threw it away. Instead of paying attention in classes, I would spend time doodling in my notebook, drawing swords, medieval creatures, and signing my name over and over.

I would question the point of going to school; none of the stuff I was learning seemed practical or useful in the real world.

That's the narrative gurus, or so called 'experts' preach these days. That you don't need to go to college and that you can be wealthy in little to no time.

While that sounds like an ideal case in a time where U.S. student loans are becoming the most prominent modern economic bubble the world has ever seen, college still has its purposes.

As early as a kid, I wanted to be wealthy. I remember sitting in the car with my family, looking out the window as we passed affluent neighborhoods.

"I want to live in a house like that," I would say, to which my father replied, "Well, you need to work hard and not be lazy."

Since I came from a middle-class family, at times, money was hard to come by. I usually didn't get what I wanted. I would see some of my classmates with the newest gadgets, and I would ask myself, "why couldn't I have that too?" "Am I not good enough for this?"

This interpretation of my youth was a constant reminder that I wasn't good enough. As a result, I grew up feeling inadequate, that I had something to prove. Particularly to my father.

It became a self-fulfilling prophecy. I nearly failed high school, and when I applied for my selected 8 Universities, all of them rejected me. I managed to get accepted into a private University nearby after taking out a substantial loan.

By then, something within me had shifted. I started to take my studies more seriously. I knew that a lot was on the line, mainly money.

I ended up with a 3.90 GPA during my first year of University, nearly a straight-A student. My father told me that if I repeated similar results in my second year, I might be able to transfer to an Ivy League University.

My parents often made comparisons between their peer's children and me, who have attended such schools. Maybe I could finally prove to my parents that I was worthy.

It seemed like I was starting to get a foothold on my life and turning things around. However, that summer, I changed my mind.

Instead of staying where I was, I left. I left my family, my home. I left the country.

That summer, I went to Hong Kong for the first time with my father. I was utterly blown away by the city. So much so that I decided I was going to move there.

The following year I transferred to a University in Hong Kong where I finished my studies at a fraction of the cost.

In pursuit of something that made no sense to me at the time. Something my heart told me was necessary.

As it turned out, as one door closed, another one opened.

My reason for writing this book

Like every book, we must have a *raison d'etre* or a reason for existence. My reason I've found is to empower others. To leave the world a better place because I showed up, and because I existed.

I hope that, after reading this book, it inspires you to look into your own life and take the necessary steps towards your goals. Even if you apply 1% of the things I share in this book, I will consider my job well done. With that, let us begin.

Chapter 2:
The Underdog Transformation

Change is inevitable. Every living being experiences change in one shape or another.

Whether you are changing schools, neighborhoods, or work, it is bound to happen. It just happened that I changed schools, neighborhoods, and country of residence all at once.

During the spring of 2011, I visited Hong Kong with my father, who was there for a business trip at the time.

Up to that point, I had been living in a bubble. Growing up in America, I never paid any attention to what was going on in other countries.

After coming back from my trip, I had to make a difficult decision. Do I stay in the US and continue my studies with the possibility of entering a prestigious university?

Or do I try something ridiculous and transfer to a university in Hong Kong?

At that very moment, something in my heart told me to move to Hong Kong. I didn't put as much thought into it as I would have liked, but I went through with it.

I bought a one-way ticket to Hong Kong and started my search for schools.

My top choice was the Hong Kong University of Science and Technology. I remember coming to the interview with a mohawk and watching as the jaws of the people in the admissions room drop. Long story short, they rejected my application.

A little while later, I received an acceptance letter from the City University of Hong Kong. I packed my bags and went on my way to study Mechatronics Engineering on the other side of the world.

That was one of the most significant life decisions I've had to make.

All of us have to face *life decisions* at one point or another. The after-effects of these decisions will impact us for years to come.

So *why* did I have to make this decision in the first place?

The answer came during a car ride on one scorching hot day in 2010. It was at least 97° F (36° C) that day. My family and I were on our way back from visiting a university in Long Island.

We were going about 70mph down the freeway when suddenly the car jerked hard to the left. My father gripped the steering wheel and tried turning it to the right.

The car then jerked to the right. I gripped the seat of my car hard. The vehicle was spiraling out of control quickly.

Everyone in the car was screaming, and I clearly remember thinking that my life was over. After what seemed like an eternity, the car then spun in a 180 arc and stopped.

In front of us was a 2-ton shipping truck speeding towards us. 40 feet. 30 feet. 15 feet. I close my eyes. Game over.

It took me a while to open my eyes again. When I did, I saw the truck. Only feet away from a head-on collision.

That was one of the closest brushes I've had with death. That experience left a lasting change on me.

That evening I went home and reflected hard on my life up to that point. I was 17, a terrible student, and if I had continued what I was currently doing, I probably wouldn't have much of a future.

Often, we have to make decisions that may seem minor at the time, but in retrospect has made all the difference.

It is just like Steve Jobs, the late founder of Apple Inc. said, "We can't connect the dots looking forward; we could only connect them looking back."

What are the experiences you've had that caused deep reflection on life?

Usually, it comes at a point of high stress in your life, failure, or disappointment.

If you cannot recall such an experience, then I'd say maybe life has been very kind to you. The only way you will break through your plateaus and accelerate your personal development would be the first to CREATE these scenarios.

I must sound like a madman right now, but I assure you I am not.

You don't grow as a person when you are resting on your laurels. Growth happens when you have to go through trials and tribulations.

If you are reading this book, I am going to assume that you've gone through some struggle growing up.

Of course, I don't advocate going overboard and trying something that might cause permanent damage.

Finding your edge

The edge is the space where you can reach your highest growth potential.

It's the goldilocks region for personal growth. Too far from the edge, and you are in your comfort zone, too far over the edge, and you are in deep uncertainty.

The edge is a space where you are pushing your boundaries far enough where you have room to make mistakes and grow.

The truth is, most people don't find their edge, much less live it. Many don't even look for it.

It takes a lot of effort, trial and error, and mistakes. You might find yourself on a dead-end road and only realize it later, to your peril. Whether or not you decide to make a U-turn and look for another path is totally up to you.

Living in alignment with your strengths can be scary at times. When you start winning, expectations begin to build. People expect you to maintain that level of growth. There is a fear of stumbling and falling short.

At the same time, the edge is a beautiful place to be. It's where you truly feel alive. *When your talents become aligned with the person you are, and who you want to represent in the world.*

To ensure you do not do something foolish in attempts to find your edge, I will share methods for helping you identify your unfair advantage later in the book.

First, let's look at the concept of 'lack' and the effect it plays on your life.

Concept of lack

Lack is simply the scarcity of some finite resources, whether it is money, time, energy, talent, or something else.

The environments we grew up in, and our upbringing determines what form scarcity takes.

I remembered when my family barely scraped by. It seemed that we were always short of money. At one point, my mother had to work in a glass factory to get some side income to help the family.

There were days she would come home with cuts on her hands from moving huge pieces of glass at work.

As a kid, I often felt that I couldn't do anything about my family's financial situation. I felt helpless as a result. The lack of money was usually the root of our problems.

There is a general misconception that "Money is the root of all evil."

The reality is, the lack of money is the root of evil. My father had to support a family of five. There were constant arguments in the household. Each time, I would ask myself, "Is it my fault my parents are arguing over money?"

Lack spread into other areas of our lives; soon, it became a lack of time the family would spend together. I began believing that everything I needed came from outside myself.

Later in life, I found that scarcity comes from within. If you feel inadequate, no matter how much money or another resource you have, you will always feel insufficient. Capital is the great amplifier; who you were before wealth will only amplify when you become wealthy.

A common symptom in the middle class is this phenomenon called 'Keeping up with the Jones.'

A man sees that his neighbor just rolled up with a new Mercedes. He might feel the need to match or outdo that, even though his barely year old car is perfectly fine.

In the end, the man tries to one-up his neighbor and in doing so, spends more than he could afford, raking up enormous debt.

Comparing what you have with others is the likely root of unhappiness and depression. Remember that you are playing your own game. What someone else has or doesn't have has nothing to do with you.

Each time you feel a void inside, ask yourself:

Are you genuinely missing something? Or do you get the FEELING that you are missing something?

A clear distinction is required.

No one can make you FEEL complete except you. Know that when you were born, you were born whole and complete. Society, through its facade of smoke and mirrors, has led you to believe otherwise.

Marketing and advertisements of slim waists, beauty skin, lean muscles, six-packs create society's definition of success and beauty.

So what does success mean then?

You are the sole person who is going to define what success means to you. Chasing someone else's definition will put you on a path to inevitable pain and misery.

You do not classify success by a number on a scale or scoreboard.

It is to be measured by the *extent that you live by your deepest values*.

Given the gravity of that proposition, make sure that you come up with the definition yourself.

Chapter 3:
Underdog's Catalyst for Evolution

Change inducting emotions

Emotions are powerful beyond belief. Some feelings hold the potential to spark lasting change in your life. We can break these emotions down between positive and negative emotions. Both kinds of feelings are essential.

People might not normally associate negative emotions as a form of inspiration and motivation. At times there's more value to gain from negative experiences than positive ones.

There's a good reason for that. We tend to remember negative experiences much more than positive ones. Think about it. I would argue it is hard to think of a time you felt extreme joy than if asked to think of a time you felt extreme disappointment or disgust.

You can use those emotions to your advantage, as fuel to get out of a rut or to make a difficult life decision.

Disgust

People don't usually associate the word 'disgust' with something life-changing, but it can be.

When something is disgusting, it's something you want to avoid at all costs.

Such as a dirty back alley filled with garbage bags. Except, in this case, disgust applies to a situation in your life.

At one point in my life, it was normal to wait beyond the usual noon lunchtime to eat. It wasn't because I wasn't hungry. On the contrary, I was starving.

The reason was that I knew that a meal cost less between 2:00 pm and 6:00 pm.

I put off eating because I was trying to save a few dollars.

One day I told myself, I'm sick and tired of trying to pinch pennies when I should be putting my focus on making dollars. I'm going to eat when I am hungry and not let this rule my life.

It was then that my focus shifted from shrinking by saving money to expanding by making more.

What part of your life is that back alley filled with garbage bags? Something that you want to avoid at all costs.

Disappointment

When was the last time you let someone down?

You told them that you would do something for them, but you never really followed through with your promise.

Disappointment from others, when vocalized, has the potential to alter your life forever.

Actively seek out feedback from people you care about because you might get blindsided to think everything is doing all right.

I've had conversations with people like David Meltzer, CEO of Sports 1 Marketing, and he shared with me the three people in his life that had a profound impact on his trajectory in life.

It came in a time where he was very successful but arrogant. His best friend didn't like the people he was hanging around, and his wife didn't like the way his ego was steering him.

The disappointment from others was enough to get him thinking about what he wanted out of life. Frustration about where you are in life is just as powerful.

If you look at yourself in the figurative mirror, and you're disappointed by what you see, that's a life-changing moment.

If you are overweight and you are disappointed in the unhealthy habits that you put yourself through, you may be spurred to alter them completely. The same goes if you are broke and tired of being lazy.

There is a real power to that. The best thing to do when you feel disappointment is to stay with it. Seek to understand what is the cause of your distress.

Only then you can find your way to move past that into something more constructive to do with your life.

In the end, with all these seemingly negative emotions comes a neutral, but mighty one.

Resolve

When you resolve to do something, you are essentially telling the universe that you've had enough. Resolve is one of the most potent emotions someone can experience.

Resolve usually follows other negative emotions, such as disappointment or disgust.

Resolve is walking into a convenience store without enough money in your pocket for a bottle of water and promising yourself you will NEVER feel that way again.

Resolve is tolling away at a job you don't like, to buy things you don't need, to impress people that you don't care for, and saying NEVER AGAIN!

Enough is enough!

Sometimes it is induced externally, but often it is an internal struggle that has been going on for a while. It may have been months or years that you have been struggling with a challenge or bottleneck in your life.

Take out a piece of paper. List the type of 'issues' that you are facing today. There is no need to be all organized about it. Just list everything that pops into your head.

Spend a good 30 minutes on it, at least.

Now with your list in mind, try linking some of the issues together.

Some of these problems you have are related to each other.

Some issues include: not having enough savings, owing money to the bank. Those are money problems. More specifically, they are income problems. Or they could be budget problems.

Other issues could be related to your health, your relationship with family, your relationship with your significant other. (or lack thereof)

Look into the root of these problems. What is causing all of it? Would you like it to be different? Are you willing to resolve never to have to be in this situation again?

Combination of emotions

When I was 14, I worked my first job at McDonald's. Aside from being the youngest guy there, I happened to be the only Asian guy. Long story short, I got picked on a lot.

Often the store was short-staffed. It was summer, and the lines ran back to the front door.

There were two people at the cashiers, taking orders. Then there was me, the only one in the kitchen.

Rotating between workstations, I made frequent trips to the freezer and washer as well as make sure all the meat was in stock and wash the excess grease off cookware.

I wore heat resistant gloves on top of latex gloves, placing hamburger patties on a 400-degree stove in the middle of July, with only a ceiling fan to keep cool.

I recalled my fingernails peeling off my fingers at the end of each day.

When the store was empty, I would change gloves, grab a cloth, mop, and bucket and start cleaning the tables and floors.

One particular day was worse than the others. Per routine, I went to clean one of the toilets. To my surprise, there was shit. Everywhere!

All over the floor, over the toilet seat, on the walls. Someone just exploded all over the bathroom.

The manager then walked in and said, "Oh shit!"

He then proceeded to hand me a tiny hand-sized cloth and said, "Clean this."

I felt disgusted. So this is what working for someone is like — cleaning up shit.

Even when I later worked in a startup environment for another company, I was mostly building someone else's dream.

That moment I resolved that I would never truly work for someone again.

Such was a life-defining moment for me. What seemed to be a terrible experience instead inspired me to do more with my life.

Curiosity

One summer, I was rummaging through my dad's basement, where I came across a box of his old books.

I was curious, so I went through the book looking for something interesting to read.

One of these books had noticeable wear and tear, yellowed pages, water damage, and wrinkled edges. What contained inside, however, was gold.

That book was called "Seven Strategies for Wealth and Happiness" by Jim Rohn. If you haven't yet read it, I highly recommend you check it out.

Published in the 80s but still relevant today. That's because the book talks a lot about the fundamentals of success, simplified to things you could count on five fingers.

There's an interesting passage in the book talking about the power of curiosity. There were four key questions.

Why?
Why not?
Why not you?
Why not now?

Want to see how far you could go and where your talents could take you?

Ask yourself these questions. If there wasn't a limit on how high you could reach, what would you do? Who would you meet? What are some of the experiences you'd have?

The power of curiosity can knock down the first domino and start a cascade, creating the momentum that you need to strive for a better life.

Passion

Passion seems to be quite a buzzword these days. People throw the word around casually, but most don't understand the deeper meaning behind it. It can be difficult to pinpoint your passion.

I believe that passion stems from curiosity and care.

Here are some questions to ask yourself.

"What is something I am inquisitive about?"

"What do I care about?"

"What would I do if money were no object?"

Better yet, "What would I do even if I wasn't paid to do it?"

Or "What makes your heart sing?"

The climb as an underdog is a long, rugged one filled with struggles. To be able to push yourself through, you need to have enough reasons why you want to do what you do.

Once you have enough reasons to do something, which aligns with your values, you will start seeing your life change.

The tide will be reeling towards you, instead of you chasing it. The reason is that you have achieved a level of clarity and certainty about where you are going. When that happens, nothing is going to get in your way to achieve those goals.

Chapter 4:
Crossing the Threshold

The Invisible Threshold

The invisible threshold is the chasm between the life you live and the life you want. Crossing the chasm is living life on your terms regardless of your definition.

As long as you're just getting by, it won't matter how much material success you've achieved. You will still compare yourself with other people's version of success.

The void is made up of your worries and fears. You are the only person that can bridge this gap and cross. It requires 100% personal responsibility for the life that you want. When you walk away from what's undesirable, you start moving towards your dreams.

Like a ship, you can't change your destination in an instant, but you can change your direction by adjusting the sail. Changing your direction happens with a single decision, which is made up of thousands of smaller moments battling with your inner-self leading up to that decision.

The Transfer of Fear

Fear is often the thing keeping us from making the lasting change that we have wanted to. Think back on the goals that you have scribed onto a piece of paper.

How long has it been since you wanted to achieve your goals? How much longer are you going to wait until you take that leap?

Fear is universal among humans. It kept our ancestors out of harm's way. It's the thing that reminds us that we are human, fragile, and capable of demise. At the same time, fear can also be something that propels us to great heights.

Take out a piece of paper and do this exercise with me. Draw a line down the middle.

On the left-handed side, write down all your fears. Some common ones are fear of failure, fear of embarrassment, fear of rejection, and fear of loss.

Lay it all down everything. Don't leave a stone unturned. There's something therapeutic about writing down the things that scare you. The aftereffect is that they become less scary.

Now on the right column, write down the 'positive' inverse fears to the ones you just wrote on the left column. You must be thinking right now that I'm nuts. How could fear have a positive side to it?

Essentially it is the side of fear that empowers us rather than dis-empowers us. To illustrate, I will make a chart of my fears:

Dis-Empowering Fears	Empowering Fears
Fear of Failure/ Mistakes/ Being Wrong	Fear of Regret From Inaction/ Things Never Done/ If Only 'If'
Fear of Uncertainty	Fear of Regret/ Things Never Done/ If Only 'If'
Fear of Rejection	Fear of Not Being True To Myself
Fear of Embarrassment	Fear of Indifference/ Obscurity
Fear of Unworthiness	Fear of Living Below My Potential
Fear of Disapproval	Fear of Living Misled
Fear of Loss	Fear of Attachment
Fear of Dying	Fear of Not Having Lived

I transferred my fear of failure to the fear of regret. There was a study done at a nursing home on patients on their deathbed, reflecting on life. They all spoke of the disappointments of things they did NOT do, rather than the things they did do.

By shifting your fear, you did not remove the fear of failure, but you _diminish_ its significance. If the fear of failure is holding you back from getting started, then the fear of regret will pull you towards taking action.

Here's another example. If you transfer the 'fear of rejection' to the 'fear of being untrue to yourself,' you might start caring less about what other people think. You might still fear rejection, but it becomes irrelevant.

Does that mean we could master our fears once and for all?

The truth is, we don't.

They say most people fear public speaking, and it's up there with the fear of death. I did. I've been speaking to audiences big and small for years. I still get nervous before getting on stage.

Fear can be supplementing fuel to help you rather than hinder you. It's the precursor to courage.

Courage is not the absence of fear. Courage is acknowledging the fear and forging onwards in spite of it.

You gain courage when you say to yourself, "I'm scared, but I am going to do it anyway."

World-class performers have the same fears as you; the only difference is that they didn't allow those fears to hold them back. They used anxiety as fuel for excellence. If nothing else will get you through hard times, courage will.

Once you make a decision, see it through. Things will happen for you that defy your wildest imagination. Many of us were raised to avoid failure at all costs.

Don't fear loss; fear not living up to your potential.

Use fear to your advantage. The privileged will fear potential failure and loss. That's because there are expectations they try to validate. If you start at the bottom, you have nothing to lose.

The Stories We Tell Ourselves

Let's face it. We all have a story, one that is factual, and one that we tell ourselves.

Were you bullied as a kid? The experience may have been a few moments or even a few years of your life. The trauma may extend far longer into your future. We may grow up believing we are weak and helpless, just like that inner ten-year-old. The stimulus has long vanished, but the sting of the pain is still there.

Until we make peace with our past, we cannot have peace in the future.

Many people hold onto their past and allow it to define their every state of being. They avoid doing things that may bring them into close contact with their past trauma.

Some never resolve their trauma in their lifetime, which is the saddest part. So much potential shunned because of the story one tells oneself.

Think back about a painful experience that you had in recent years. This exercise may prove challenging to some, as we desperately try to suppress these fragile memories.

Think long and hard about the facts of this experience. Some of these experiences never actually happened. What do I mean they didn't happen?

There are the actual events that happened; then there's the story we tell ourselves about what happened. We cannot trust our mental capacity to remember the exact truth of events that have occurred.

Often, we make up details in our minds about what happened, a mere construct of our imagination. We remember the emotions associated with the memory, but we may be amplifying the effect it had on us.

What we give power to is what ultimately controls us.

We become victims of our own story. We seek acknowledgment, sympathy, and pity from others.

When we embrace our story and let go of the need for validation is when we start living fully.

Take out a piece of paper and write down a personal story that comes to mind. Write down as much detail as you can recall. Include how you felt about the experience, then and now.

What are some of the ripple effects that have perspired into your daily life based on that experience?

Are you afraid of starting your own company because of something you failed at during your childhood?

Do you sometimes feel unworthy of success because someone important in your life made you feel like you didn't deserve to win?

Once you have written everything down, read it out loud. After you have read the entire story once, do it again. And again.

Don't stop reading it until you're tired. Physically and mentally exhausted. You will notice that you start to become sick of the story. When you become tired of repeating the same experience over and over in your head, you begin to look for a solution. Once that happens, you have the space for acceptance.

Accept and make peace with your story. Vow to not allow the experience to hold you back from living a life that you want for yourself. At first, this may seem very difficult. You may have been telling yourself this story for many years.

It will take some time. Acceptance is not a one-time thing, but an everyday decision.

Practicing Acceptance

We all have activities we do to avoid reality. Things to feel good about ourselves. Activities like eating, drinking, sex, drugs, and video games. It's part of our coping mechanism as humans.

We need to practice acceptance so that we can take full responsibility for our lives.

We all wished for more: More money, more time, more of X. When we get it, we want even more. It is a never-ending spiral to oblivion. There's nothing wrong with desiring more. The key is to be able to appreciate what we already have. We can escape the moment temporarily, but we eventually come back to where we started. This means that in order to move forward we need to accept the past.

Of the four pillars, the Physical, Mental, Emotional, and Spiritual, the Spiritual holds a particular purpose. It provides a more meaningful sense to the other three components.

We can practice acceptance in the form of meditation by spending 10 minutes alone in your room every day.

Sitting still in a room by yourself and doing 'nothing' is probably one of the hardest things to do in modern-day society.

We live in an age of distraction. If it's not our mobile phones that has our attention, it's something else. If you resist sitting still, finding peace becomes infinitely harder.

Once you are sitting alone, close your eyes. Rest your hands by your sides. Inhale for four seconds. Now hold your breath for seven seconds. Finally, let your breath out for a count of eight seconds.

This process is known as the 4/7/8 breathing cycle. It is designed to help you relax.

You might notice a lot of noise buzzing through your mind. Allow yourself to be. Accept all the thoughts that come and flow through you. Be at one with your thoughts and emotions.

You will realize that it isn't that hard to do. The activity itself is natural. Humans make it difficult.

That's because humans are always trying to make sense of why they are doing something. It sounds contradictory to what this book is about, which is about living your purpose.

It's known as duality. For the sake of simplicity, understand that both conditions don't exist without each other.

To get closer to our purpose, we must first let go of the idea of searching for it.

Our purpose lies no further than ourselves. The only thing left to do is uncover it. To do that, we must let go of our need to search.

Don't beat yourself up over missing a day of practice. I know it was something I had to overcome. I was my worst critic. Every time I finished a speech, I would always think about how I could have done it better.

People are coming up to me, telling me that I did great. You see, that was the story I told myself. The idea that I wasn't good enough.

It stemmed from my interactions with my parents when I was still in school. They would usually scold me for my bad performance. The conversation wasn't whether or not I had tried my best, but rather why didn't I get an "A."

Lasting transformation is a process, not a destination. Be ready to spend a lifetime practicing. In the meantime, your inner demons will try to exert control over you. Over time, they will weaken.

They never truly go away, you just get stronger.

Letting go the Need to Be Right

Everyone, on some level, wants to be right about something.

One of the hardest things I've had to do was shut up when someone was clearly in the wrong. Letting go of the need to respond or correct them was painful and excruciating.

The more you think about it, the more the idea of staying silent might make sense to you.

What's the point of being right? You might feel good about yourself at the moment. What about the cost of being right?

It's easy to go and correct people for their faults, instead of looking within and facing your most deep-seated evils. The latter is much harder. Before you go trying to fix other people, work on yourself.

It runs even deeper than that. What do you desperately want to be right about with your life?

Holding onto half-truths keeps us from meaningful self-development. It's limiting at best and delusional at worst.

The process of identifying things that no longer serve us, and deciding what we delude ourselves with is both a liberating and necessary step in our evolution as humans.

Crossing The Threshold

At one point, you have to decide to cross the threshold between the life you used to know and the life you want for yourself.

It starts as a commitment to yourself that you will do whatever it takes to succeed as long as it is legal and ethical. There is no real 'secret' behind it. Nothing happens until you pull the trigger and take back control of your life.

It might be walking into your bosses' room and handing in your resignation letter. It might be resolving to never work for someone again. It might be walking away from a toxic relationship that is consuming your energy and attention.

There will never be a perfect circumstance or sign that tells you it is the right time to burn the bridge. As cliche as it sounds, it is what it is.

The majority of us are hoping for a miracle to fall from the sky and save us — a silver bullet. *The only miracles are those we create for ourselves.*

Be ready to deal with potential consequences; it's a question of whether you are willing to embrace the uncertainty.

Be ready to live with your choices for every victory also incurs a loss; for every loss carries a blessing in disguise.

Chapter 5:
The Three Questions for Lasting Change

Before we commit ourselves for change, we must first ask a variation of these three questions.

1. Who do I have to be able to live the best version of myself?

Do. Have. Be. A majority of people get the order wrong.

Most believe that either: They need to have resources so that they could do certain things so that they can become successful.

Or they need to do certain things so that they could have material processions and resources that will allow them to become who they want to be.

The reality is that the answer is: 'Be. Do. Have.' We must first become the kind of person that would do the tasks necessary that will get us what we desire.

What kind of traits must a bodybuilder embody if they want to get their body in the best shape possible? They would need to have discipline in their daily regime, what they eat, how often they exercise, etc.

Mediocre people will believe they either have the genetics to become fit or they need to invest in some expensive equipment or meal plans, or other' shortcuts.' Without the traits of a successful bodybuilder, no supplement or external resource can get you sustainable results.

2. What needs to die inside me so that I can live my best life?

The lack of self-awareness holds us captive. We need to let false beliefs die within us. To rewrite our script of the future, we will need to drop the doubts, fears, and worries of the past.

3. What do I need to let go of so that I may achieve my goal?

There are a lot of things we hold onto for dear life because we are uncertain about the future. The more you hold onto those things, the more those things hold onto you.

It might be a job that you are struggling to quit. You know that you aren't treated right there, it's not providing any upward mobility, but it also feels secure. Therefore you find yourself stuck in inaction.

It could also be a toxic relationship that we are in. We refuse to cut ties out of the fear of being alone. In doing so, we become more dependent on the other person and the relationship, which doesn't seem to have any positive future for you.

Commit to becoming the best version of yourself. Demand that your life is a message for the world. Let your actions speak volumes where your words won't.

Chapter 6:
The Art of Unlearning

"Listening to classical music can make you smarter."

"We only use 10% of our brains."

"Thomas Edison invented the light bulb."

Chances are, you've probably heard at least one of the above. These statements might sound logical and may even pass as conventional wisdom. The problem is that all of those statements are false.

Dr. Alfred A. Tomatis's "Mozart effect" was a theory that claimed that listening to Mozart, the famous 18th-century classical composer, would make you smarter. Except there was no definite proof that classical music would have a lasting mental improvement on the brain.

The idea that we only use 10% of our brains was perpetuated and re-enforced by popular culture and Hollywood films like *Lucy* and *Limitless*, where the protagonist in each film was able to harness superpowers by employing more of their brain's capacity.

The truth is that our brain is 2% of our body's mass, yet uses 20% of our body's energy. As for utility, in an interview with Scientific American, Dr. Barry Gordon, a neurology professor at the John Hopkins School of Medicine, mentioned that humans use "virtually every part of their brain."

Finally, the last point may come as a shock. After all, didn't our science teachers in elementary school teach us that Thomas Edison invented the lightbulb? There were many iterations and permutations of lightbulb concepts before his time. The only difference is that his version of the bulb proved "practical, and affordable, for home illumination."

Conventional wisdom has time and time again proven to be misleading. The narrative to become financially successful used to be to go to a good school, get a high-paying job, climb the corporate ladder, and reach the pinnacle before retirement. Indeed, that is one way to do it, but it is not the best way for everyone.

Earlier in 2019, 16-year old Kyle "Bugha" Giersdorf, made headlines when he walked away with a USD 3 million check after beating 99 other competitors in the popular online multiplayer game, Fortnite.

How about Evan, the kid that reviews toys on the video-sharing platform, Youtube, under the username 'EvanTubeHD,' which has made him over USD 1 million annually from ad traffic? By the way, Evan (last name withheld in all interviews), is only fourteen years old.

There are countless other examples of individuals without a high school diploma, who have completely transformed the way we view making a living as well as life.

Which begs the question, *what other 'facts' do we know about the world that no longer serves us?* o

The idea never really occurred to me until I had to 'unlearn' what I thought knew about the world at 19. I felt that New York City was the center of the universe, that all opportunities to get ahead must come from there. It's the city that never sleeps, right?

I was wrong about that too. Little did I know that Asia was a rising giant, with opportunities that would allow me to grow faster than if I had stayed in the U.S.

After coming to Hong Kong for the first time and having my eyes opened, I had to rethink what I thought to be true for my current reality.

It was common for people to eat 'siu ye' (宵夜), short for a midnight snack in Cantonese, until the wee hours of the morning, where most Americans would probably be fast asleep.

Then you have karaoke goers finishing up their evenings at 6 am, and street peddlers setting up shop just before the sunrise. Hong Kong was indeed one of the many cities that never sleep.

Within a few years of coming to Asia, I found myself in the same room as executives and C-suite officers from multinational companies. That would seem unheard of in the U.S, but it was possible in Asia.

It's not an argument of where is an ideal place to work and live. Instead, it highlights realities that we have accepted as gospel without questioning its impact on our worldviews.

How we see the world changes our reality. The same for the questions we ask ourselves.

What reality have you accepted, for a fact, which drives your existence?

In answering that question, we must follow up with a similar question, *what must I unlearn to move forward in my life?*

There's a plethora of information in the world. There are 152 million blogs on the internet. Guess how many websites there are? Over 1.8 billion!

With the scale of information outflow, we face a daunting problem. What's accurate, and what's speculative? Whose advice do we take?

Sources state that to lose weight, you must cut carbs (ketogenic diet). Other sources say that you can eat however you like but at designated periods during the day (intermittent fasting). Other sources say dieting doesn't work, and that you have to focus on fixing your sleep.

If we blindly follow advice from the internet or others, without questioning whether it fits our life, we will metaphorically be 'spinning our wheels' or doing a lot of things but going nowhere. It's like being a hamster on a circular wheel; no matter how fast you run, you will still be in the same place.

Similarly, if we follow sound advice with conflicting values or belief systems, we are fated either re-evaluate our world view or accept defeat.

If you find yourself in a tight place, perhaps it's not the method that's keeping you stuck. There's a lot of techniques that work and will get you to your destination. It might be the reality that you have accepted for yourself that no method will be able to help you get out of.

Let's take the example of dieting. Regardless of which one you try, if you are prone to try something for a while and change it up if no noticeable results surface, then it's unlikely any diet will help you.

The issue isn't the method of diet. It's your approach to taking action that's holding you back. This behavior will show up in other parts of your life. It will show up in your relationships and work.

You will dip your toes in the shallow water and retreat when things don't work to your liking.

Another example is the idea of liking and disliking specific tasks. That was one of my biggest struggles when it came to working on my own business. I enjoyed working my own hours and having the freedom to do what I wanted whenever I wanted to do it. What I didn't like, however, was doing admin work, waking up according to schedule, and keeping a routine.

I was a mess without the typical wake-up, go to work, come home, and sleep routine from working in a job. That's when I realized that I lacked discipline.

If you are starting your own business or venture, you might find yourself working on tasks that may seem minute, especially ones that don't contribute to the bottom line.

Whether or not you like it, unless you go and hire someone to do it, you're going to do it.

When tax season came around, I had to present my company's accounts and records to the accountant. Since I had a habit of not being on top of my bookkeeping, the files were a mess. It took a lot of time, money, and effort to fix the problem.

My relationships and health also suffered due to my lack of discipline as well as likes and dislikes. I was single for four straight years due to being extra picky about who to date. I also had nutrition deficiencies because I didn't particularly like eating fruits, which gave my body the proper vitamins it needed.

Something that I've learned over the last couple of years was that '*how you do one thing is how you do anything.*'

How you approach one aspect of life also shows up in other parts of your life.

Learning to do things required of me, whether or not I enjoyed doing it, was something I had to unlearn. Guess where I got the idea of only doing things I enjoy? The internet.

I sold myself on the idea that to be a successful business owner, I needed to outsource things that weren't my core competency and focus on my strengths.

Even though it makes sense to specific situations and people, such as those with traction and resources in their business to delegate their efforts, it doesn't make it a universal principle.

That said, don't take anything you read in this book or any book at face value. The idea is to ask whether it applies to you.

Even if it does, you also want to ask yourself whether your beliefs and ideas that hold you back from making use of the advice.

There might be learned junk from your past that you may need to unlearn in order to apply the new knowledge.

What's Next

There's a lot of advice out there, how can we determine what is useful for us, and what is just noise?

The next part of this book is dedicated to auditing your skills, and piecing together the resources that will help you break free of your circumstances.

I'll be pooling my experiences as well as the experiences of those I interviewed for this book to bring you the best insights in taking your life to the next level.

Chapter 7:
Overhauling Your Inner Circle

Your Inner Circle

You have probably heard that you are the average of the five people you spend the most time around.

If your inner circle is broke, chances are you are broke as well.

If your best buddies go out every weekend to drink and party, chances are that you do too.
Humans have an intrinsic need to find a sense of belonging. In doing so, we knowingly or unknowingly create tribes around who we are.

Write down the names of your closest friends. What are their interests? What kind of hobbies do they have? What topics usually come up in conversation?

You will realize that you have so much in common with them.

Along your journey, there are going to be those that don't understand your ambition. Those people will try to unravel your plans by trying to poke holes in it. Over time they will pull you down to their level. Sometimes those people are those we care for deeply, parents, relatives, and siblings.

They mean well, but they are probably not the best people to help you reach the next level.

Your immediate circle of five is probably one of the hardest groups to reconstruct. It's difficult to walk away or spend less time with those that have been around for a long time, but don't let time fool you.

They may have been childhood friends, college friends, and so forth. Know that you may have outgrown them and need new friends.

Those that will inspire and help you get to the next level.

Reshaping your Circle of Influence

To change our level of influence, we must first change our circle.
There are a few steps of reshaping our circle:
Elimination, Re-Enforcing, Addition, in that order.

Take stock of the people in your life and their level of support towards what you. Pick out one or two people that have always been there for you and fully support you.

I was fortunate to have parents supportive of my work. It came after years of rebellion and after leaving home for seven-plus years.

You will face a difficult decision, which is to cut off all the people that don't support your hopes and ambitions. No matter how long you have known them. We should not use time as a metric to judge other people's support and intentions for us.

Some have known us for a few weeks with better intentions than those that have known us for years. Hold in your mind the idea that you may need to cut someone out of your life at any moment.

Make a list of five people that you need to spend less time with, or need to eliminate from your life. This period of cleansing is painful but is necessary, and you will start to see results that spout from this exercise.

The second step is the reinforcement of positive relationships that are going to take you to the next level.

It might be a mentor that you have been meeting for an hour every three months. It might be a friend that is a great listener and supportive of what you do.

Make a list of five people that you want to spend more time with and reinforce your relationship.

Finally, we will replace the five people we have eliminated with people that we want to spend time with, but haven't had the chance to yet.

These are people that are potential mentors, clients, or any other person worth associating with. Social media provides an excellent platform for you to do research. Keep stock not just what the person does, but also what kind of person they are. Do they have traits that you are trying to cultivate? Are they in an industry you want to get involved in?

People make the mistake of only expanding their network before either eliminating or reinforcing people in their pre-existing network.

Your attention is finite. It is challenging to maintain a massive network and juggling other priorities without wearing yourself thin.

Building Your 150

Dunbar's number, proposed by British anthropologist Robin Dunbar in the 1990s, states that a human could maintain and manage roughly 150 stable relationships before cognitive breakdown.

A majority of people do not consciously manage their network, which is a big mistake. I would break down the network of 150 as such.

1. Your Inner Circle (5)
2. Your Strong Ties (45)
3. Your Weak Ties (100)

Your strong ties are solid relationships that you have with others, where there is know, like, and trust factor. You would typically speak with these people at least once a month.

Your weak ties consist of acquaintances that you may contact or see once every quarter. Although the name seems to suggest otherwise, weak ties are usually the ones that will open more doors than your inner circle.

The people on this list could include mentors, successful people in your industry, and acquaintances you have connected with but haven't had the time to build a deeper relationship. Weak ties can often serve as a bridge between you and someone generally out of your reach.
What's more important than your goals is realizing who can help you turn it into a reality.

If you're willing to spend a few hours crafting a list of people that fit into these three categories, you are well ahead of most people.

Who do you have to meet to make your dreams become a reality?

I would suggest coming back to this list at least once per quarter as things are bound to change.

Schedule a time every month to ping people on your list, whether a text message, a phone call, or e-mail. Look for ways to add value to your interactions. The best thing to do would be to meet in person and build up your relationship further.

Equally as important is to have people in your network of 150 that come from a variety of fields. I would challenge you to include a few people that are from completely different walks of life. Include people that live in different cities or countries as that would help you broaden your network significantly.

The Importance of Finding Your Tribe

First off, what is a tribe?

Since the dawn of humanity, tribes have been essential. It stems from a deep physiological human need. On Maslow's hierarchy of needs, it fits into the need for belonging.

One of the basic human needs is the need for belonging.

We all want to find a place where we belong. Thousands of years have passed, but the need remains the same.

Instead of traveling nomadically from place to place within a single tribe, we are now part of multiple tribes.

With the internet, we have even more choices that were previously not available. Geographical location and lack of digital communication separated our ancestors. Conversely, we are free to roam the world with a plane ticket or the internet.

Tribes have far-reaching implications that penetrate the vast majority of society. The last few decades presents an opportunity that has been mostly absent in modern civilization.

In the past, if you were born into a poor community, it would be a challenge to break out. A community has its way of keeping you in line.

Some communities are not only physically dangerous but psychologically dangerous. Imagine growing up in an environment where the average education level of its occupants doesn't pass high school.

What motivation does one living there have for higher education? What support will one receive if they want to strive for more?

The most vulnerable communities of all, however, is in front of us.

It's called 'middle class'. The middle class is the spawn of mediocrity, another word for average. Why is it dangerous?

It's because many are conditioned to believe that getting by with average is okay.

Unlike the more impoverished communities, middle-class communities generally do not face dire hardships that inhabitants from the former face every day.

It can't get any worse for many of the poor; they could only go up. There have been many individuals that grew up with nothing and were able to create massive success.

They make a significant impact on our lives because they were able to overcome all odds and breakthrough despite the odds.

Then there is the other form of underdogs, which are those who have grown up in reasonable, not dire environments, whose families have gradually risen to middle-class status. For the most part, they have stayed there with each passing generation.

The Power Of Communities

If you attend networking or community events, you will notice that you are the unknown figure wandering the venue, either by yourself or with a friend. You could be among potential clients and may not even know.

Often the setup of the event may prevent you from having an in-depth conversation with new acquaintances. At the end of the evening, everyone leaves with a bunch of cards, but barely any real connections.

That said, you are better off creating your community where people can bond. There are a few critical advantages that you have when you are a leader of a community.

1. You are an authority figure

As an attendee someone else's event, unless you're an 'influencer' or 'thought leader' in your space, you will probably be invisible to most. This dynamic completely changes when you organize events. As an authority figure, you could attract high-quality individuals, often those more successful than you. In an instant, you gain authority and credibility with everyone present, something difficult to establish otherwise.

2. You are the event host

As the host, you carry a lot of responsibilities such as: organizing the event, booking the venue, recruiting participants, collecting money, and other small tasks.

You get a chance to be in touch with all the participants ahead of time and curate your event to match the community ethos. As the host, it is effortless for you to network as well as connect with others. Learn a bit about each person beforehand. Find out who is in a similar field or has similar interests and introduce them. People will thank you for that as they are getting value from meeting like-minded people.

3. People Sell You Instead

Not limited to physical events or functions, it could also come in the form of knowledge sharing. You can come in as a teacher, educating your audience on your expertise. In this way, you do not need to sell yourself. Instead, people will approach you to inquire for more.

Now that you know the benefits of starting a community, how could you get started?

The first step is to establish the target audience and theme that you want the community to be centered around. Ideally, this is a niche community. Niche communities focus on serving a particular demographic and interest.

I'd first picked up golf through a mentor. It sucked playing by yourself; therefore, I was looking for other people around my age that also played. I realized two crucial details: many ex-pat golfers in the city left their clubs to gather dust, and all the other golf communities in the area targeted people over 40.

Therefore I decided to start a Meetup group (meetup.com) for working professionals in their prime or under 40. By narrowing down my audience, our organization was able to appeal to people that shared a similar interest (golf) with the same problem (no like-minded people to play with).

By starting a community, you will instantly boost your credibility, authority, and expertise in your field.

Chapter 8:
Finding and Creating Leverage
As the Underdog

The Great Plateau

Many first-generation immigrants from China, South Asia, and Latin American settled down in America back in the 60s, 70s, and 80s. They came to America with mostly nothing to their name but willing to work for everything.

Their children, the second-generation, were born around the 80s up to the early 00s and raised during a period of historically low crime rate and peacetime. A time where the internet became widespread and mobile phones became mainstream.

This my generation, dub the Millennials. A Millennial (or Gen Y) is simply someone born between the 1980s and the early 2000s.

Millennials have started to question their purpose or reason for existence. In their parents and grandparents' age, there was only one objective. Their role was to work, make money, and provide for the family. In today's technological world, the younger generation has so many options available to them.

With the aid of the internet, Millennials have grown up with an unmatched level of wealth around them. During their childhood, they were more financially comfortable than any generation before them.

Because Millennials got all of their basic needs met in their youth, they seek to get their psychological and self-fulfillment needs met. This is why Millennials struggle with a purpose or rationale for their purpose in life.

In comparison to the older generation, they have simply developed different values about what is important in work and life.

Nowadays, if you were born with enough food on the table and content in your sleep, you begin to strive for more than just money.

You might want to find work in something meaninful. Success might not mean how much money you can make, but the impact that you can make on the world.

Millennials have faced lots of criticism as of late. We are labeled entitled, spoiled, lazy, among other things.

Speaking for the broad spectrum of Millennials, I know that to be untrue. I've known many Millennials that put in the work and hustle several jobs while paying their way through university. Some even ran companies while they were in school.

There has never been a time in history where an individual has so much power over their destiny.

With the internet and a mobile phone, one could access an infinite resource of information and reach virtually anyone influential on planet Earth.

However, with such power and choice of options, many times, we are stuck on what to do.

How does our environment heavily influence our choices?

As a second-generation Chinese American, I grew up in an immigrant family.

While my father never attended high school, he educated himself after work every day, and managed to be the first person in our family to attend a university.

For him, success was the only option. There wasn't a luxury of choice, given his environment and circumstances.

While growing up, I would often get nagged by my parents, like most of us. They wanted me to do well in school and possibly secure a good-paying job.

The career expectation for a lot of Asians typically falls into three popular fields. Either an engineer, doctor, or lawyer. Nowadays, banking is part of this list.

Although they have our best interests at heart, they may encourage us to pursue careers and work that do not align with our deepest values.

Many of us face this dilemma. It's not a time to resent our parents or lash out at them for not understanding us.

Instead, we should take a moment to appreciate that they do this out of love. They do not wish for us to struggle and hurt the same way they did.

They only wish we live a better life than them. It's only rational for them to suggest safe and conventional routes.

Now let's look at this from a community perspective.

Generally, similar social-economic groups tend to band together. In New York, you will see large communities of Chinese, Korean, Vietnamese, Latino, living in with their own. Your neighbors are likely to be from similar backgrounds.

Can you see why it would be complicated for someone to be an outlier and pave their road?

Research shows that people mostly stay within a 50-mile radius of where they were born. That's the power of community; it can work in your favor and against you.

The inertia of defying your parents and relatives is one thing, but to go against the grain and do something that virtually no one in your community is doing. That's very hard. The support isn't there.

At least not in the beginning.

When I started on my journey, I also faced a similar struggle. The realization hit me hardest when I encountered hardships.

On the surface, it is a reasonably big problem. What made it worse is that I had to face my parents, my relatives, and my community.
Personal embarrassment for me wasn't enough; I faced public humiliation.

People around me got to say, "I told you so."

It was a way for them to assert that they were right, or that they knew better.

Academics is something taken very seriously in Asian culture. At a family gathering, one of my relatives told everyone that my cousin was accepted into an Ivy League. She then turned and asked my parents the same question.

The expression on my parent's faces said enough.

At that moment, I resolved that my parents would never have to feel that way again. It's moments like those that change us forever.

We avoid making mistakes out of the fear of failure, messing up, or looking bad. The reality is that many of the successful people you see, and there were no smarter than us. They are just as flawed as we are.

Once we have these experiences, they present us with an opportunity to break free from our circumstances. Events that seem like misfortune may be a blessing in disguise.

Look around you. You may notice that some of the people you grew up with, went to school with, your best of buddies, may not be the people that will help you get to where you want in life.

If the people around you prefer to work in stable companies, at permanent jobs, it will seem strange to them that you are trying to work for yourself.

Some may feel insecure that you are pursuing your own goals and ambitions and try to pull you down. They will say things like "it can't be done" or "that doesn't seem like you."

It's difficult to understand a reality so far removed from them that they will try to justify their reasons for staying where they are.

At the same time, with society rapidly changing, it's more dangerous to stay in one place than adapting.

We were born to manifest greatness, yet so many allow their surroundings and circumstances to dictate their destiny.

The decision that you will not stay where you are. The commitment to see it through. The persistence to weather the battles, trials, and tribulations. Only then will you be able to expand what is possible, as an underdog, as a human being.

The 5 Levels of Leverage

Once we have committed to improving our lives, what now? We have to obtain something called leverage.

The word 'leverage' is interesting. If you deconstruct it, you have 'lever' and 'age.' Quoting Archimedes, an ancient Greek mathematician, physicist, engineer, inventor, and astronomer, "Give me a lever long enough and a fulcrum on which to place it, and I shall move the world." How can we incorporate this into our modern-day society?
If you have finite resources, which is the case for most people, you can make up for intangible skills or assets. These are what I call 'levers.' The levers will help you rise from where you are, as it has for me ever since I moved to Asia without a dime to my name.

By learning the skills and creating the assets outlined in this chapter, you will be very far ahead in your market, in your space, and your competition.

The longer the lever, namely, the stronger you are in a particular skill outlined here, the more leverage you will be able to generate in your life.

Here are the five power levers.

1. Network/ Circle of Influence
2. Leader of a Community/ Organization
3. Public Speaking
4. Sales
5. Personal Branding/ Marketing/ Positioning

In no particular order, these skills help you generate substantial leverage in your career and your life. Your network and circle of influence will help you open doors otherwise tricky to access.

Being a leader of a community will make you an authority figure in a domain and attract people to you instead of having to go to them. Public speaking is one of the essential leverages because it provides you a platform to make your voice heard.

Sales skills are also crucial because everything in the world revolves around sales and marketing. The ability that you have in convincing people to buy from you will significantly impact your success in the long run. Personal branding, marketing, and positioning in the market is an excellent trio as it can help you expand your reach.

Public Speaking

I used to hate speaking in public. The very thought would terrify me.
That was until I had to confront my fears after giving a presentation in class in high school. It took time, but I slowly began to enjoy it. Shortly after I came to Hong

Kong, even while in university, I went looking for opportunities to practice my public speaking skills.

One of my most memorable speeches was to a crowd of 30 people. To me, it wasn't the number of people in my audience. It was the fact I was speaking at a university that had previously rejected me. I was talking about entrepreneurship to students that could have been my peers.

My public speaking skills took a turn for the better when I joined Toastmasters, an international organization for public speakers, and started participating in speech competitions.

There are many resources out there to improve your public speaking, joining speaking clubs like Toastmasters is just one of many.

Sales

The ability to sell is a form of influence. From the being of humanity until the present day, everyone is in the game of sales and influence.

Either you are influencing others, or others are influencing you.
Not being able to sell effectively is going to create a lot of hardship in your life.

The world economy relies on sales. Without sales, there wouldn't be money to keep the lights on, to keep providing service to customers, and keep people employed.

The most important sale is YOU, the sale that happens no matter where you go.

By now, you're aware that everyone on planet Earth is a salesperson. It is the great equalizer.

It doesn't matter where you come from if you can sell your ideas, you give yourself a way to make a better life for yourself.

Elevation

To elevate is to uplift yourself or others to a place where they previously haven't been. Growing up, I was obsessed with trying to find ways to improve or elevate myself, whether it was through books, audiobooks, conferences, seminars, or mentors.

It wasn't until the last two years that I wanted to elevate others.
The real measure of a leader isn't the competence you exhibit. Although we like to think so, most people do not care what's going on in your life.

They are thinking about themselves. So the idea that you need to get to a certain level before people see highly of you is absurd.

Instead, if you elevate or lift those around you, you will slowly amass a loyal following that is willing to help you bring an idea into reality.
If you place your focus on helping others achieve their ideals, they will, in return, help you achieve yours.

It all required the little efforts of those around them, knowingly or unknowingly. The greats will acknowledge this much.

When you invest your time, energy, and entire being into the pursuit of something worthwhile, you will find those willing to tag along.

They aren't necessarily there for the novelty, and chances are they aren't there for you. They are there for what you represent and the vision of what you are trying to call into reality.

Chapter 9:
Winning the Game of Life

The Game

Life is just a game of people. Not in the sense where you play with others to merely get what you desire, but it is a maze where you need to navigate to your destination.

There are levels to the game of life. Everyone you meet will be in a different chapter of their life. At each stage, various things are required of us to progress to the next level. What got us where we are now might not get us to the next level.

The transition requires a different kind of thinking, approach, and methodology.

I believe that winning at life isn't based on external representations of 'winning.' From the outside, we may vaguely guess that those that are more financially well off than us are living better. While that may be the case in semantics, the real answer is within.

The person you think is living great may disagree. In their minds, they may be losing. Let's say they are the owner of an 8-figure company, which by no means is a small amount. However, the owner feels they won't be successful unless they hit 9-figures. It could be due to expectations, internal or external driving their feelings.

Or due to feelings of unworthiness, inadequacy based on someone else's metric.

For the longest time, my metric for success tied to my father. To me, he was the embodiment of a 'rags to riches' story.

To get to where he is today, he went through a lot of struggles and suffering. In that sense, I tied the struggle and pain to success. I would look up to those that went through hardships and became wealthy in their own right.

Deeply embedded in my psyche was the need to struggle or suffer.

My father never required me to go through the ordeals I put myself through. The whole point of working so hard was so that I had a life better off than he did.

It's a habit of Asian immigrant parents, don't praise your kids, for you don't want them to be intoxicated with their success.

The worse thing they become arrogant and complacent.

As a result, life became this series of struggles for me. I didn't need to spend four years living next to a funeral home, with cracked ceilings, a moldy bathroom, and fake floor tiles.

I was living, or should I say, reliving my father's life through struggling.

I was recreating it artificially to prove a point.

What that meant was if I wasn't successful, that means I didn't suffer enough. Often, as humans, we have a habit of wanting to prove ourselves right.

In this case, I was sabotaging myself.

Procrastination, laziness, distractions seemed to consume my days. Which would prove a point that "you know what, you're not worthy of success."

In reflection, I realized that to break the cycle, I have to sever my spiritual connection with my father, so that I may live my own life.

It doesn't mean for me to renounce him or rebuke him. It means accepting that I will never outdo his struggle and win his story because that is solely his.

For me to move forward, it means writing my own story. It doesn't mean that I won't have struggle; it just means I won't be seeking it out as a way to success.

Ultimately, it allows me to take back control of my life. For everyone, it is different.

Everyone carries with them an invisible burden from the past. To move on with our lives, we must first uncover, discover, acknowledge, and accept those so-called 'burdens.' In doing so, we free ourselves of the weights chained to our feet.

It took me a long time to step out of my father's shadow. When I look back into the past, I realize there's nothing there for me.

It's like grasping onto sand; it slips from our hands. We give away our power to our pasts, trying to 'recreate' someone else's and not live ours.

When we look out and make comparisons, there is no way we could win.

When we look within and find our best, our self-worth, we begin to reclaim our power. It has never left us. We have just forgotten about it. I would say we misplaced it.

Most people dim their inner greatness. Don't let that be you.

Allow my story to be an example of moving into, through, and past the attachment to other people's expectations for you. Make a conscious choice today that you will start living for yourself.

Life is not a game to be mastered. Quite simply, the purpose of life is to create an experience that you want.

The more you look within, the more you will see that it's not that hard to dance amid chaos and thrive.

Creativity

Creativity is often talked about, and as an underdog, it is critical.

Creativity will help you get out of your current situation, however unfavorable. It will give you a competitive edge, or what I would call an 'unfair advantage.'

We don't try to compete with people with more resources than us. We probably won't win that way.

David did not take on Goliath head-on, nor will we.

We don't need to do what everyone else is doing, which is going through the front door.

That includes blasting your resume to dozens of companies, cold calling prospects, and trying to stand out at a networking event.

Most people follow this route. That is because none of those actions and activities require creativity. To truly stand out, what's needed is creative thinking and planning before taking action.

When we get motivated or excited about a new opportunity, there is a tendency to blindly charging in. Yet that may not be the optimum way forward.

Winning Conditions

It is essential to establish 'winning conditions', which are contributing factors to success at any endeavor.

When your plan aligns with the winning condition(s), you are more likely to accomplish your goals.

Winning conditions appear in almost any conceivable game ever created. In basketball, the winning condition is to score more points than your opponent team by the time the buzzer rings in the 4th quarter.

In a business deal, the winning condition is that you have satisfied your company's objectives, while also meeting those of the other party.

Regardless of what activity you partake in, there are winning conditions. Winning conditions encompasses every decision and ordeal we decide worthy of commitment.

3 Steps to Using the Win Condition to Accomplish Goals

1) establish what the winning condition is. It will help you determine if accomplishing set tasks will get you closer to your personal goals. Distractions arise when you don't know your true objective.

In the latter case, you will merely be drifting along, winging it, and sometimes getting lucky. Other times, you will bite off more than you can chew.

2) start plotting your plan for executing, setting benchmarks and milestones.

Each benchmark and milestones must be aligned with the win condition and your end goal. Both must be quantifiable.

3) be aware of indicators showing how far or close you are to your goal: Keeping track of how far you are from the winning condition will ensure you are focused and not succumbing to shiny objections that pop up from time to time.

An unconventional truth

Let's be honest.

Certain goals sound great at the moment, but soon turn out to be a huge distraction.

I've been heavily distracted over the last couple of years. Back in 2015, I was obsessed with becoming a digital nomad.

The idea of working from anywhere in the world, without a boss, building my own business was very attractive to me. It was like a breath of fresh air to the 9 to 6 that I was supposedly "stuck at."

The digital age can have an intoxicating impression on our psyche. We see people on channels like Instagram, Facebook, and Youtube living their "best life" while we are quietly hating ours.

What does "living your best life" mean, anyway?

The phrase is thrown around casually by people that probably don't understand or know what it implies.

They think it makes them sound cool when the phrase is just another vanity measure of life.

Traveling the world, eating well, partying every night at the trendiest spots in town doesn't necessarily mean you are living your best life.

It could simply mean you were running away from your old life.

I'm not saying that you shouldn't experience this at some point in your life.

Life is much more than posing in a picture to look cool in front of your followers and to make your friends jealous.

I would know because I was one.

When I left my job and started traveling the world while running an online company, I thought life was spectacular.

I had saved up around $30,000 from my previous two jobs, and it was expected to last me at least nine months with little to no income.
It was enough to get me going. The idea was that I'd be able to start producing enough revenue in 9 months to fund my travels and lifestyle.

To my surprise, the fund would end up lasting close to 15 months.
For some time, it was the most euphoric feeling in my life.

I got to spend time in New York with my family. I saw them more in 3 months than I had ever seen them in the six years I was living in Asia.

Over a period of 12 months, I got a chance to go jet skiing in the Bahamas. Scuba diving in Cebu. Kitesurf in Boracay. Watch the Formula One races in Monaco. Backpack in Japan. Live a month in Taipei. Two weeks of Muay Thai camp in Chiang Mai as well as a dozen other trips spanning several continents.

The experiences were exhilarating, exciting, and no less than impressive. After a while, it got exhausting. Exploring the world was exciting; working wasn't.

Packing light was liberating on the back, but the burden of expectation was heavy on the heart.

After visiting all these places and more, I began to reflect on the emptiness of my journey.

I remember standing across Lake Kawaguchi and absorbing the splendor of Mount Fuji, Japan's most massive mountain.

It was mid-April, the cherry blossoms had just come out. Arguably the most beautiful time in Japan. It's where millions come to enjoy the first blossoms of Spring. A cool gentle breeze was coursing through my hair.

There it was, the totality of bliss. It was also at that moment that I felt a void in my heart.

Months leading up to the trip, I was working on numerous things, in attempts to make money, and keep my lifestyle going.

I was going on Instagram, telling people how great my life was. When in fact, it was far from that. In my attempts to find meaning, I lost sight of my North Star.

I had no idea what I wanted to do with my life.

On camera, it looked like I had my shit together. When in reality, I was alone, bitter, and sad.

The traveling began to feel empty. Constantly moving from one city or country to the next. Not only was I physically exhausted, but I was also mentally and spiritually drained.

Travel was supposed to be something to look forward to, to be enriching, and enlightening. At one point, it became meaningless.

I was spending so much time thinking about the photos and videos that I wanted to capture for my audience, that I forgot to actually capture the moment and live in the present.

Without that, life was truly fleeting. Distractions came in abundance: drinking, women, gambling.

All the vices came out at once because I didn't know what I wanted.

I was running away from it all. Travelling was just my excuse. I was lying to myself, telling myself that my life is fantastic, when in fact, it wasn't.

I was not just running away from my expectations. I was running away from my potential.

I had put this artificial pressure on myself. I was still trying to recreate my father's life someway, somehow. Artificially create suffering and struggle. So my lesson here is quite the unconventional one. It's one social media influencers won't tell you.

When you chase artificial success and 'feel good' moments, you are selling yourself on an illusion.

That illusion will only erode and siphon the life out of you. It will turn you into the worst version of yourself.

Don't make vapid trappings of success your goal. Set goals that you actually will be proud of achieving.

When we are born, we are given at least two gifts. The first is the gift of life. The second is the gift of talents.

The second gift is the one you give back to the world through actualization of your talents.

The gift of talents is one that is often taken lightly and taken for granted.
That's where entitlement comes in. We believe because we were given such talents, on some level, we deserve to get better treatment. That life should be more comfortable for us.

When we get stuck there, we are held captive by our arrogance. As a result, we don't truly strive for our highest potential.

The Pain of Ignorance

Most of us would like to think we are rational, where our judgment is sound in spite of external evidence suggesting otherwise. It makes for an argument that we know what we are doing.

We flaunt some indicators of success to the outside world, telling others not to challenge our fragile state of existence.

An existence we have spent little time pondering and even less time examining.

It gives us a way out. To not have to go through the act of asking (or answering) the hard, challenging questions.

Questions like, *"Why am I doing what I am doing?"*

"Why am I living the way I am living?"

"What is an ideal worthy of aspiration, even if it might not materialize?"

"What am I lying to myself about?"

"Am I living according to my values or the values of others?"

That is because it would call into question our so-called rational thinking mind, which has long been influenced by forces outside of ourselves.

Subliminal forms of neuro-programming that fade into the background, making lasting impressions on our malleable psyches.

To challenge our actions and decisions would derail the narrative that we know what we are doing. Our emotions heavily influence a majority of our rational sounding choices. The pain of ignorance claws deep into us.

It is annoying at best and morally excruciating at worst to not have an answer to life's problems.

The ability to sit without an answer is way harder than dismissing the question entirely.

I would make a plead that it is necessary to examine our lives.

To have the courage to look into the dark corner of our very being, and slowly remove the blinds that block the light that shines within us.

When things don't work out as you've planned, dare to look within, rather than point fingers and play a victim of circumstances. Have the courage to look yourself in the mirror and own up to yourself.

To change the world, start with changing yourself.

Before we do that, however, we need to resolve the battle that all of us go through.

Stepping out of the shadow

The process of stepping out of the shadow of your past may take years, even decades. For some, it is a lifelong battle without any end.

Most people lead their lives without awareness that they are stuck in someone else's shadow. They try hard to prove someone wrong.

Yet they can't ever seem to get that satisfaction. Every new accomplishment feels fruitless and empty. Nothing ever seems to be enough.

In that context, nothing will ever be enough. That's because you base success on someone else's reaction to something you did. Therefore, don't depend on someone else's recognition or validation.

It will never fill you up like the recognition and validation you give yourself.

People such as world renown speaker, Rapid Transformational Therapy trainer and best-selling author, Marisa Peer has devoted their lives to helping people break the cycle of feeling inadequate.

One of the methods she recommends to her clients is to look in the mirror every day for 21 days and say this one phrase.

"I'm enough."

By repeating this phrase over and over again, they are reprogramming their minds. Soon enough, they will start believing those words.

I'd like to take the process one step further.

A friend of mine suggested this practice after I shared my experiences of not feeling worthy.

She said when you go to the mirror every morning, and tell yourself three things.

I am proud of you, Gilbert, because ...fill it in.

I forgive you, Gilbert, for ...fill it in.

What I am committed to you Gilbert is.... Fill it in.

The practice had lasting impacts on my day-to-day life because of the importance of each of those phrases.

Let's take the 'I am proud of you' line first. It means that you are acknowledging, recognizing, and appreciating yourself. Self-praise that we often deny ourselves.

We tend to focus on the next thing, without stopping for a moment to congratulate ourselves.

"What are you proud of yourself for?"

It doesn't have to be something significant. Woke up early today and exercised? Great, acknowledge it.

Got everything on your task list completed the previous day? Give yourself a pat on the back

Next off, "What I forgive you for." How often do we forgive ourselves? Chances are probably minimal. We are usually beating ourselves up for little things that happen every day. When we do that, it's hard to feel good.

More importantly, we must learn to forgive ourselves for our mistakes. Forgiveness is like the calm breeze that sets upon you when you are in a quiet place, entirely at peace with yourself.

When we practice forgiveness daily, we gain a better perspective on life. Although we screw up at times, we accept it and move on. It is much better than bottling it up inside until it explodes.

Finally, the last statement, "What I am committed to you" is about the future.

Now that you have acknowledged praised, and forgiven yourself, what's next.

What are committed to creating today in your work, in your relationships, for your wellness?

This question reminds you of your vision and what you were put on this Earth to do. It does not include playing small.

This practice changed my life, and it will change yours. Start today, do it tomorrow, and soon you will become second nature. Miss a day? Don't worry, get up and try again.

Sooner or later, you will reap the benefits of this simple exercise. Free yourself of your past darkness.

Greatness By Default

I believe that greatness is in all of us, even if we don't see it.

Along your journey, you will also encounter people that see it before you do. Recognizing your greatness is a long but fruitful journey.

Doubts are plentiful, and there have been many nights where my mind was down in the dumps. From the outside, it looked like everything was okay.

I was "traveling the world." I had the freedom to do things wherever and whenever I wanted. At the same time, my inner struggle was a lot more revealing.

The self-talk begins the negative spiral downwards.

I had a typical case of imposter syndrome. Imposter syndrome is the feeling of inadequacy in spite of continued success.

Even the greats have admitted that they sometimes feel doubts of their own greatness.

It led to this personal realization that you earn your greatness — every single day.

Just because we are now on top of the world does not exempt us from demanding more from ourselves.

Those that rest on their laurels will lose it all. What holds the power to create also holds the potential to destroy.

What you do with your gifts is totally up to you. We are simply the sum of a lot of small decisions and events adding up.

It's normal to attribute success to significant events that occur or big decisions that we make.

If you think about it, you could probably count the number of significant decisions you ever made on the one hand.

University or no university?

This industry or that industry?

Quit your job or stay?

Keep running your business or throw the towel?

Who to marry?

Kids or no kids?

For some of us, we may use up to 2 hands.

Between these big decisions are many, much smaller choices.

The results of all those smaller decisions also influence our more significant decisions, for better or worse.

There aren't that many big decisions that will require your attention. It's the little decisions that trip you up.

Of course, you may say, but if I quit my job now and start my own business, it might be a big mistake.

It doesn't have to be, though. If you build a strong foundation beforehand, then you have a much better chance of justifying significant risks.

For example, when Bill Gates, the 2nd richest man in the world, decided to drop out of Ivy League university, Harvard, and start Microsoft, a world-renowned computer company, many would have called that crazy.

In Bill Gates' mind, that probably wasn't the case. He had accumulated enough programming experience to build the first product for Microsoft.

He was probably also aware that if the venture didn't go as planned, he could always go back to school.

If he stayed in school, he might have missed that window of opportunity that he had at that moment.

It was the coming together of preparation and opportunity. For most people, that would be a risky ordeal.

Once we know a bit about the little decisions made before that, then we can understand the bigger picture.

Therefore, in a world of imperfect information, we usually can't predict the consequences of our big decisions, but we can prepare to handle them better by making enough little decisions.

Positive EV decision making

In poker, EV is the short form for expected value. EV measures the likelihood of a positive future results.

Let's say you roll a six-sided dice. There are six sides. The chance of you throwing a specific number is 1 out of 6 or 16.7%. You have a chance to win $100 if you roll a 5. Otherwise, you win nothing. To play, you need to pay $10 per roll.

So would this be a good wager?

16.7% to win $100
83.3% to lose $10

That makes the reward ratio 10/1. Which would be a fair wager because, in theory, you could roll six times, lose $50 and win $100, for a net profit of $50.

The idea is to take risks that do not outweigh the potential benefit.

Making more positive EV decisions over the long run will change your life's trajectory dramatically. The problem is many people don't make enough decisions. They make the same big decisions we all have to make at some point, but in-between they shy away from mini-risks.

The more times we put ourselves at-bat, the better the chance of scoring a home run.

Increasing the volume of small bets you make will, therefore, increase your preparation for life's big decisions.

Each of these small decisions is:

- Measurable in risk/reward
- Quantifiable in targets/ outcomes
- Aligned with your larger purpose in life

Let's go more in-depth on how to measure decisions with favorable outcomes.

Tim Ferris,' the author of 4-hour workweek, talks about this in his TED talk where he mentions Fearsetting.

Fear setting is the idea of imagining your worst possible outcomes for taking a course of action.

When we are locked in indecision, usually it comes from the fear of the unknown. The fear of uncertainties, uncertainty, ambiguity, or volatility. In management, they refer to this as VUCA.

'Fearsetting' will highlight potential outcomes, potential negative consequences, and rank them. A '1' means that the worst possible outcome is minimal, while a '10' would irreversibly alter your life.

Fear setting is a great exercise that I recommend for everyone. After spending 30 minutes, you'll see that the negative consequences are not as dramatic as you might imagine.

Most negative consequences are probably registered a 3 or 4 on that scale, meaning you will be back on your feet in little time.

When I made my jump from my job straight into being a digital nomad and starting a business, I had $30,000 in my bank. After 15 months, I was dead broke, and three months after that, I was in debt.

I didn't get the financial payoff, but I gained a lot of life experience.

It took a year to recover; therefore, my risk was kept to a minimum. Looking back, it wasn't so bad.

As the old saying goes, you could always make more money, but you won't get your youth nor your time back.

The thing is, we usually work with limiting information. Therefore, it is essential to do a risk assessment before committing to a course of action.

At the same time, it's challenging to make real life-altering mistakes. It's far easier to make positive life-altering changes.

Before we make our decision, however, we must weigh our risks properly.

Weighing Risk

When it comes to life decisions, we need to factor in the age of the person when they make that decision.

The older someone gets, the less risk they tend to take. Present an opportunity to someone at 25 and someone at 40, and you will have different considerations.

For example, starting a business out of university is relatively low risk, as there is almost nothing to lose. If five years go by and the venture ends up a failure, you will have gained invaluable experience and still be in your 20s.

Whereas if someone has a family, kids, a mortgage, and is thinking about quitting their job and starting a company at 40, the risk is much higher. If the venture fails, it may cause lasting damage to the family's financial health, relationships within the family, and even health problems.

Someone at 40 may have accumulated more valuable experiences to apply to their business, which is also an important factor to consider.

The smaller decisions leading up to a big decision makes a huge difference. Those decisions could reduce the financial risk of failure, such as having proper financial planning in place.

It could also amplify their chances of success. Imagine they were able to meet top talent willing to come on as a co-founder and secured potential investors before making the jump.

We should not get too over eager to try a new opportunity because someone was able to become a millionaire in less than 12 months.

We shouldn't be discouraged if we are told that the chance of success was less than 3%.

Statistics show us one angle, but the small day-to-day decisions provide an even better perspective.

When we can combine the insights from both perspectives, we can begin to make better decisions.

Chapter 10:
Controlling Perception
with Questions

So you have decided to ascend your limitations. To step out of your past and into your greatness.

Where do you go from here? How do you get out of being an underdog?

Once you reshape how you see yourself, you need to reshape how the world sees you.

When you control other people's perceptions of you, it becomes much easier to open doors that would otherwise be closed.

Look at two scenarios.

Person One hasn't shaved in days. They are wearing worn-out jeans and dirty shoes.

Person Two is wearing a custom-tailored suit. Their shoes have a fresh coat of shine on them.

Both of these people walk into the same party. How do you think they will be treated?

The second person, in the absence of any other distinctions, will be taken more seriously.

The way we present ourselves, how other people perceive us has a significant effect on what doors end up open to us.

People's perceptions of you are not limited to what you wear. It has to do with how you stand, talk, gesture, and carry yourself.

Social elements also play a big role. If you meet someone for the first time through a mutual contact, it's going to have a different effect than if you met them as total strangers.

The good news is that most of these elements can be positively influenced and controlled.

I remembered what it was like when I was a naive kid without any resources, without any idea what to do to stand out. Trust me, it sucks.

Controlling the perception of others may sound manipulative, but it isn't. Everyone is trying to show their best version of themselves, whether knowingly or unknowingly.

It is better to put your best foot forward without being manipulative, disingenuous, or dishonest.

So how does it work?

For example, I love to talk. If you find me in a room filled with people, it is effortless for me to make conversation. From the outside, you might see me as a super extroverted person, but in fact, I'm not.

I enjoy spending time by myself. There are some days that I do not want to talk to anyone. I even enjoy watching movies by myself.

The most significant difference is that I can show my true authentic self WHEN I do mingle with people.

I would reveal both my strengths as well as something vulnerable about myself.

When you are vulnerable, you allow people to lower the walls they use to insulate from others.

The walls come from their inner struggles and their past traumas. You are not there to resolve them. However, you can bypass them by using strategic vulnerability.

By sharing something personal and meaningful to you, you open the channel for connecting with the person.

People connect through vulnerabilities. No one likes someone that only shows their best. It brings out other people's insecurities, and no one can relate to a "god-like" figure.

So what do you share to disarm people's natural responses strategically?

Question Banks

People have natural responses to canned questions, or questions that people gravitate towards when meeting someone new.

Examples include: "What do you do for work?" or "Where are you from?"

People have been asked these questions many times before, therefore they will default to a handful of responses. Those responses may or may not inspire new or interesting conversations to follow.

Questions allow you to empower others to share information, thoughts, and feelings with you. It will enable you to understand their concerns, needs, and desires.

We can use questions to find out more information, clarify what was said, mirror what the other person has said, handle objections, and screen intent.

Each type of question gauges the rapport that has been created and has the other person increase their investment in connecting with you.

Time and time again, many successful people have told me this golden piece of advice.

If you want to get a better answer, ask a better question.

It is easy to fall into default modes of thinking and acting. You ask the same outdated questions that don't get you anywhere.

Questions like, "What do you do?" Or "How do you do?" Or "Where are you from?"

As a result, people will respond with canned answers.

Rapport isn't a destination to be reached, rather a process both parties engage in. Therefore, a great question will make someone snap out of their preoccupation.

When that happens, the chance of being remembered is much higher. A question bank is a collection of high quality, thought evoking questions.

Let's face it; when asked generic questions, we sometimes give "fake answers." As a way to brush off the question entirely. When that happens, you lose an excellent opportunity to make a solid impression.

Instead of trying to fill in the silence, involve the other person to fill it with something meaningful. See yourself as the coordinator for an interaction, whereby the question is like a guide for creating a quality interaction. There are many kinds of questions that you can ask.

Clarifying Questions

Clarify questions are straightforward and simple questions used to clarify a fact or statement. People often give vague answers, depending on the kind of question asked.

If you want to understand someone better, you might want to clarify some of the things they tell you. It's a form of probing for details without making them uncomfortable. Make sure you know what someone wants and for you to be useful.

Also, it is common to assume that we know what other people mean through our frame of reference without trying to understand the definition of the topic from their point of view.

What are some examples of a clarifying question?

"You mentioned that you are looking to work towards your dream of starting your own company. What does that entail?"
"You said you want to be successful. What does success mean to you?"

In a sales context, here are some questions you might ask.

"Does this fulfill the objective and help you solve the problem? If not, what would do it?

"You said earlier that your wife, who is not present today, may have some concerns. What kind of interests do you think she would have?

"On a scale of 1 to 10, 10 being exceptional, what would you rate this solution to your problem? What would make it a 10?

Clarifying questions have a broad range of use in day to day interactions.

If no clarification is needed, but you want to probe deeper, one of the best ways to do it is through these three words:

Tell me more.

That alone will get people to open up and share more.

Mirroring/ Empathy questions

Next, we have mirroring questions.

Mirroring questions are non-directive, which serve a particular purpose of encouraging someone to elaborate on a previous statement or to confirm a fact.

It is also an excellent way to show empathy towards something that matters a good deal to someone. You confirm that you are taking the time to understand who they are and what their needs.

People can be vague at times when they reply. You can dig deeper and root out uncertainty by asking mirror questions.

When you mirror someone, don't just paraphrase what they said; inject the emotion that you believe they're feeling.

Here are some examples of mirroring questions.

"So what I hear is that you are in between jobs and it's been frustrating, is that correct?" "

"What it sounds to me is that your relationship with your wife hasn't been so well as of late. How does that feel?"

When you mirror someone, you invite the other person to go deeper into what they are experiencing.

Regardless if it is something positive or negative, there is an invisible wall holding people back from sharing something personal. People are afraid of being judged. They are worried about what people might think if they open up.

Through vulnerability, we genuinely get to know someone — the feeling of being real.

Mirror questions work best after you have gotten to know the person a little and want to take it further. They seem like someone would like to associate with, work with, or befriend. Namely, you want them to be in your life.

Screening Intent Questions

To get a better idea of whether someone would be a potential friend, business partner, or client, you screen for intent.

Showing intent does not mean commitment. It's merely the first step of the process.

If you are a salesperson or entrepreneur trying to get a sale, you must first screen their intent of purchase before getting them to commit.

You want to screen for a prospect's intent to purchase as well as root out potentially hidden objections.

There are many ways to phrase such a question depending on the objective. You phrase these questions by asking 'how.'

Here are a few examples:

"How do you intend to move forward?"

"How do we proceed from here?"

"What do you believe are the next steps?"

"How do you see us working together?"

"How do I gauge your commitment on this?"

Screening intent is good at the later stages of an interaction, particularly if something that involves both of you collaborating or if a sale is to take place.

Overall your question bank should have a good mixture of all 3 of the different kinds of questions, all for different stages and situations.

The same way that questions apply to your interactions with people; it also applies to your life.

Want to change your life? First, change your questions.

Chapter 11:
Controlling Perception with Stories

Story Banks

A story bank is a collection of your personal stories that you can use when interacting with people.

Why stories?

People have told stories since the dawn of time. That is probably not going to change. That is because the way our brains respond to stories is different from how they respond to words and raw information.

The brain has some essential organic chemicals or hormones that get released based on different stimuli.

The first one is cortisol, which is the stress hormone. It is released into our blood when there is anxiety, distress, or something that draws our attention. It keeps us alert and on top of things.

When we tell engaging stories, we aid in the minute release of cortisol in our audience that will keep them hooked and attentive.

Then there's dopamine. Dopamine is associated with the brain's reward mechanism. Every time we see, hear, or feel something desirable, we get a small hit of dopamine.

Think of social media. Each time there's a notification on our smartphones, there is a tendency to check it and see who has liked or commented on our social media posts. Each time we receive one, we get a potent hit of dopamine.

It feels good and sends a signal to the brain that it's pleasurable every time a notification pops up. It's why people are so attached to their smartphones; it is the ultimate dopamine machine.

When we hear a well-crafted story, dopamine is released to keep us hooked because there is a reward to be had for continuing to listen on.

According to the Zeigarnik effect, proposed by Russian psychologist Bluma Zeigarnik, people remember incomplete or interrupted tasks more than they do complete tasks.

How that relates to stories is that we try to manually fill in the blanks for the questions in our mind about it.

Then we have oxytocin, which is responsible for forming social bonds between people. It invokes a feeling of empathy.

When a character in a story goes through a setback, we show empathy towards that character, especially if we previously had a similar experience.

Finally, there's serotonin, a chemical associated with the feeling of happiness. A good story gets messy in the middle but usually has a happy ending, which aids in the release of serotonin. That feeling of euphoria passes onto your audience.

So the purpose of story banks is to create a collection of your best stories, crafted to deliver a specific message, or invoke a particular emotion.

Story banks are usually used by public speakers when they have to piece together a narrative in a short time or speak on their feet.

A story bank is a useful asset that will be invaluable for life.

The best part of it is that it is unique to everyone. Everyone has a unique set of stories that make them who they are.

Here is a simple guideline for picking and crafting your best stories.

C- Customisable. How in-depth you go in your story depends on who you meet and how much time you have to share the story.

R- Repeatable. The story doesn't lose its effect from repeated exposure.

V- Versatile. The story is suitable for many different occasions.

H- Highlight. The story highlights certain positive qualities about yourself, without self-proclaiming them.

T- Timely. The story adapts to a particular circumstance, situation, or occasion. In other words, it's related to the conversation.

There's a nominal duration for each story; you don't want to ramble. You risk losing the audience's attention. Nor do you want to over-simplify the story and leave out essential details. A well-balanced story would be roughly 2-3 minutes.

How many stories should your story bank have? A healthy story bank would contain at least five carefully crafted stories. You should have 10-15 minutes of stories to tell, which weaves into your conversations.

You might have a lot more different kinds of stories to tell, which are situational. The more stories in your story bank, the more versatile you can be.

Done correctly, you will leave a positive impression on your audience. People can relate better to you, especially if they have had a similar experience. They are also more likely to trust you since you shared something personal about yourself.

Qualities that would otherwise be hard to demonstrate on the spot like courage, persistence, grit, passion.

Early in my career, I was networking with people older and more successful than me. Sharing stories allowed me to bond with them.

Whereas everyone else was trying to impress with their credentials, I was trying to form genuine connections through sharing a piece of my life with them.

In turn, you will encourage people to share a piece of their life with you. When they do that, you will also get to know them better and be able to identify their qualities, wants, needs, desires, and pains.

The funniest part is that I often see people talking about how great they are, but rarely take the time to get to know the other person and figure out what makes them tick.

How to Tell a Great Story

Stories have been around since the dawn of humanity. Tribes used to gather around the campfire and share tales and stories.

Stories engage the part of our brain that relates closely with emotion. It links our rational (newer mind) and our primal brain.

Therefore, we tend to remember stories, whereas we forget facts and figures.

A good story has a few crucial components.

1. Purpose

Why are you telling the story in the first place?

A story without a clear message will not fully be able to serve its purpose. Therefore, before picking a story to tell, identify the core message of the story.

2. Vivid Imagery

How do I effectively communicate this message in the story? What are the details you need to include for the audience to get your message?

Too many details will overwhelm your audience. Too little, and you risk being vague. A good story has just enough vivid elements that paint a picture of what's happening in the story to the characters, setting, plot, and conclusion.

The best way to part a vivid picture is to use imagery words like, 'cloudy', 'warm to the touch,' 'plush-like,' 'blissful,' 'gut-wrenching', 'thirst-quenching', 'exquisite,' and other colorful descriptive words.

Try using a thesaurus to find substitutes for less colorful words like, 'good,' 'bad,' etc.

3. Backstory

How developed are your characters?

There's a good chance that you are the main character. Sometimes you are retelling someone else's story. Regardless, have a backstory leading up to the main plot.

The backstory gives the audience context into the kind of person you are and influences that you've had before the events.

4. Structure

What is the structure of your story?

Without a structure, you risk going off on tangents and start talking about other things that are not relevant to your main plot.

A well-structured story has a backstory, the rising conflict, the climax, the falling conflict, and the conclusion.

With this format alone, you can turn events into stories by just plugging in each element.

5. Delivery

How will you deliver the story?

Good stories are told,' great stories 'are relieved.'

Great storytellers can relive the moment with their audience, no matter if they share the story once or a thousand times.

Make sure your gestures, emotion, tone all match the story when you relive the story. Have you ever been told a story and gotten goosebumps or butterflies in your stomach?

That's the effect of great storytelling. Don't just retell your stories. Relive them.

These are the fundamentals of great storytelling. With a bit of practice, you will become an expectational storyteller in no time.

Through stories, you can reveal your own needs and allow the other person to help you. People that are arrogant and appear perfect repel help because, from the outside, they have everything handled.

My advice, don't be one of those people.

People will sense your good intentions and desire to help you in return.

Chapter 12:
Controlling Perception
with Analogies

Analogy Bank

Another secret tool you can use to master persuasion is an analogy bank. Where a story bank is a collection of your best stories, an analogy bank is a collection of your best analogies.

See what I did there?

I made it easier to grasp a concept by juxtaposing it with another idea that is easier to understand.

By doing that, I make it easier for you as the reader to be on the same page as me with the least amount of effort.

It is a very effective way of explaining things concisely without using many words.

Brands use this as well. They make their products synonymous with other well-known brands.

For example, in Silicon Valley culture, to explain crowdsourcing platforms, founders would say they are the Uber for X.

Airbnb would be the Uber for apartment rentals. Since people are familiar with Uber and what they do, it is easier to leverage that to explain something else.

Imbuing objects with meaning

You can easily take an object and imbue it with elements of a complex concept.

For example, let's take the concept of being a giver versus being a taker. You might say that being a giver has to do with helping people, doing more for them. Whereas when you are a taker, you are always looking for what's it in for me.

Sure it's not difficult to understand, but with an analogy, it makes everything even more straightforward.

Here is a better version.

You see this glass of water here; it is essential to all life forms. I believe everyone's life represents a glass.

Some people add water to other's cups, while some drain from their cup.

When you add water to other people's cup, you nourish your relationship with them, whereas when you repeatedly take without giving, the relationship will die of thirst.

Do you want to be the one who adds to people's cup? Or do you want to drain their cup?

Everyone is capable of both. The quality of your life, the quality of your relationships depends on your *choice*.

Which one will you choose?

Boom!

Which one sounds more persuasive?

Analogies are potent instruments that could craft powerful and inspiring messages.

Used correctly, it's the equivalent of adding rocket fuel to your car.

Analogies can borrow from other people and other examples that you come across. Every time you see something inspiring with an analogy attached, clip it. Save it in your archive folder.

Collect inspiring and persuasive uses of analogies and adapt it to your message. You could use it to introduce yourself. You could use it to sell a product, a service, ask for investment, and so forth.

When you imbue objects with meaning, people come to associate that object with a story, a message, and an emotion.

Words

"Words can have power, and words are power." These were the words of Mohammed Qahtani, 2015 Toastmasters World Champion of Public Speaking.

In his winning speech, he demonstrates the value of using the right words, spoken in an effective manner that causes the audience to agree with what was said, regardless of whether it was true or not.

When you learn to speak in a manner that is both empowering and persuasive, you will be able to harness the power of real influence.

Although words are useful, they only account for 7% of communication with people in person.

Tonality and the way you say it takes 23% of that pie, while body language is a whopping 70%.

Humans are, by virtue, a visual species. We make associations with images, and it is much easier to show something than to try to explain it.

When you can make your body language match the way you speak, along with your words, you can effectively command the language of influence.

I've learned that the best way to make people remember you for a particular personal attribute, use a prop.

A physical prop could be seen, touched, held, and of course, remembered. The visual part of our brain is different from the auditory portion.

Therefore by engaging both the visual and auditory, you are allowing the person you speak with to engage more parts of their brain, which will help them recall and remember you.

Each prop can be assigned different meanings. For example, if you are in the wealth management field, and your expertise is helping your clients prepare for a rainy day, your prop could be a piggy bank.

You can easily explain the importance of preparing for a rainy day by presenting the piggy bank and using that to explain your rationale.

Take your prop to all your meetings. Let people associate that object with you and what you represent.

Better yet, one of the great ways to take up that mental space in prospects mind, send over your prop.

It will cause intrigue and interest. Since it is physical and takes up space on desks, there's a good chance the receiver will be looking at it a few times a day.

One of those days, they will reach out to you to find out what is the rationale behind the prop.

You can then refer to your story bank to sell yourself while using the prop as a way to anchor what they are feeling.

Chapter 13:
Becoming Memorable

You have to make yourself memorable, but not to the point of standing out like a sore thumb, meaning you need to adapt to the environment.

In terms of dress code, the recommendation is to dress half a step above what everyone else is wearing.

If everyone is business casual, in a dress shirt and jeans, distinguish yourself by wearing different colored shoes. Dave Kerpen, the Chairman of Likeable Local and New York Times Best Selling Author, says that his favorite color is orange.

At each event that he goes to, he will wear an article of clothing that is a sharp contrast of orange.

Humans are used to a routine, people wearing a specific uniform to work, and a range of what seems to be acceptable.

When you have a distinct piece of attire, you draw attention to yourself, but pleasantly.

It makes people wonder, inspires thought, and is memorable.

Being distinct is not limited to what you wear. You can also distinguish yourself through your style. The way you talk (confident), your posture (straight), the way you shake hands (firm), and so forth.

With time, we all deliver a sense of personal style, making this topic quite complicated.

The whole idea is not to try and be like other people, regardless of how successful they are.

There may be things that you emulate, but to copy would make it superficial and unnatural for you.

Have you ever walked into a room and seen someone conduct themselves with elegance, grace, and pose?

That is because they are comfortable in their skin. Most people, by the way, aren't.

Feeling comfortable gives you an advantage over those that are nervous and fidgety.

Well, what if you are in a room filled with confident Type As?

Well then, once again, only your unique style will allow you to shine out. That will put you into the Top 1%.

You can begin to notice the results almost immediately.

People seem to treat you "better," and it's a result of you seeing yourself in high regard.

It is a simple 'life hack' but the effect ripples across and compounds with time.

Sooner or later, you will find yourself hanging out with those that you previously thought were out of reach. Doors seem to open for you. Of course, the struggle isn't necessarily over.

You still need to work hard; that's a given, but the payoff of a few simple changes makes a huge difference.

Before we can move on, we need to revisit the Five Power Levers and associated limiting beliefs that hold us back from our greatness.

Limiting beliefs that stop us in our tracks

Sales

As mentioned earlier in this book, sales are one of the Five Power Levers that will allow you to get to the next level in your business and life.

Changing the perception of people towards you, telling stories, imbuing communicated values through the use of props are all forms of selling yourself.

The most important sale you will have to make is selling yourself. No matter your standing in the world, you need to sell yourself.

Are you applying for jobs? You need to sell yourself.

Are you selling products? You need to sell yourself.

Convincing someone to go on a date with you? You need to sell yourself.

Some people hate the word sales. It gives them a picture of an old school salesperson with slick hair going door to door.

Therefore, it is one of the limiting beliefs that keep them stuck in one place.

The reality is, to get ahead in life, you need to embrace the idea of selling.

Another limiting belief is the need to build up your brand, whether online or offline.

Some believe that it is tacky and artificial to build up their brand, that those who do it are fake.

While there are people that are fake and artificial, most people with a strong personal brand are generally authentic.

Again, it's about amplifying your strengths, revealing your vulnerabilities, and fully embracing who you are.

By doing so, people will see you as authentic, no matter how much you amplify your positive points.

You're showing that you aren't perfect, but someone relatable and trustworthy.

These two limiting beliefs hold us back from putting our best foot forward and selling ourselves. They hold us back from breaking our plateaus.

The process takes time, but here's an exercise you can do to breakthrough.

Exercise #1

Make a one-sentence pitch, a 30-second pitch, and a 2-minute pitch about yourself.

Some people find it easier to start with the 2-minute pitch and work down to the one-sentence pitch, while some prefer to start with one sentence.

Regardless of preference, this exercise will help you gain clarity on adding value to others.

By nailing these pitches, you come prepared for any opportunity that presents itself, leaving nothing to chance.

Best of all, each version allows for varying degrees of engagement.

When you meet someone, and you're short on time, use the one-sentence pitch. If done correctly, people will ask you to elaborate, to which you can expand your thoughts to the other two pitches.

The 30 sentence pitch is usually the elevator pitch, because of the time it typically takes to get from the ground floor to a target floor in an office building.

In reality, you may find yourself on a line waiting for food and end up speaking to the person in front or behind you. In that situation, the 30-second pitch would be perfect.

Better yet, if it is in an environment where you could instantly go and sit down (like a cafe), then you'll get a higher chance of leaving a positive impression.

None of the pitches need to be inflated or artificial. Keep it clean, concise, and engaging.

Exercise #2

This next exercise has to do with personal branding. The next time you attend a function or dinner, dress half a step up from the expected dress code.

Once again, you are putting on a signature or "attention-grabbing" accessory. It doesn't have to be flashy; all it has to do is to convey your unique personal style.

For example, I wear glasses everywhere I go, but not just any pair of glasses. My frame is unique; the front is a single piece of titanium. One side is shiny, and the other has a matte finish.

It gives me a sort of futuristic look like someone tech-savvy and sophisticated.

You may need to do some experimenting to find what accessory fits your style. A general rule of thumb for the different kinds of accessories include:

- Bracelets
- Earrings
- Hairpins
- Belts
- Watches
- Ties
- Tie clips
- Pocket squares
- Glasses
- Hats
- Scarves
- Even the color of lipstick

Of course, there are other pieces of clothing you could experiment with, such as the color of your shoes, suits, jackets, and more.

All of these add to your style and enhance your brand by giving you a form of distinction from everyone else.

It can be a reasonably straightforward exercise as you don't have to DO anything. You need to add a signature item to your attire. The rest is all observation.

Exercise #3

The last exercise I am going to suggest is an observation exercise.

This exercise is also very simple and straightforward. Here's the thing, though.

What is easy to do is also easy not to do.

It involves going somewhere upscale, ideally out of your comfort zone. Getting a coffee, or drink and sitting alone.

You are then spending the next hour or two just observing your surroundings and taking notes.

It's like an MBA class in human behavior.

Observe how patrons talk to each other, how they dress, treat the servers, and conduct themselves.

That will teach you more than any book ever will.

For you to gain success in your life, put yourself in an environment where others are already somewhat successful.

As Tony Robbins has said over and over, "Success leaves clues."

Follow the trail.

Ask yourself why those people are doing what they are doing. What does their behavior say about them as a person?

People that go to those places have grown attuned and refined towards that kind of lifestyle. Modeling successful people is nothing new. When you are out doing this exercise, seek to model what works for you individually.

You won't need to change who you are to start going where you want to go. You need to change some of your habits by observing and modeling people who are where you want to be.

Spending one hour per week at an upscale establishment is enough to pick up your set of clues. Each time you complete the exercise, go back home, and reflect on what you have just seen.

Pick just one positive thing you have observed and commit to incorporate it into your daily life.

Whether that is a simple hand gesture, a way of standing, touching the back of someone's elbow when greeting, the list goes on.

You will find yourself with a high level of awareness of what's going on around you. This skill usually takes years of practice to master, but you can get very good at it after a month or two of deliberate practice.

Chapter 14:
The 3 Power Levers

Public Speaking

They say that among the top fears that people have, number 1 is not death. It's public speaking.

To an extent, I will agree with that. When I was getting into public speaking, I would get bouts of anxiety before every speech.

People want others to like them. They don't want to go on stage and freeze up or say something wrong.

Public speaking didn't come naturally to me at first. I stepped out of my comfort zone regularly.

I would say the same thing for writing. It didn't come naturally to me; I had to work on it over and over until I got it down.

The most significant benefit of public speaking is to be able to amplify your voice and message to more people.

Therefore, by not improving your public speaking skills, you are ignoring a great deal of potential.

The good news is that if you can overcome this fear, you will be well ahead of most people who wouldn't even dare try. It's all about looking for ways that will help you stand out and move up while amplifying your power.

Networking

NThe word 'networking' gets a bad rap these days.

I remember when I started my first company and attended a "networking mixer." After telling a headhunter what I did, he said in a condescending tone, "good luck with that."

Chances are, if you attend events, you will meet your fair share of aggressive salespeople, headhunters, insurance agents, and unemployed.

You will most likely not find any suitable candidates for your circles of influence at a regular networking mixer.

Those mixers had specific groups of people in mind. They are usually free to join; therefore, they are easily accessible. When that happens, the likelihood of you meeting someone of high caliber is low.

After a while, people will say, "Networking doesn't work for me."

To an extent, it doesn't work. Not in the traditional way of doing it anyhow. The whole idea is to get yourself in an environment that allows you to meet other high-quality individuals.

The people you want to be meeting get dozens of event invitations on any given evening. You can be sure they are not attending networking mixers to kill time.

If that's true, how can you get in front of the right crowds?

First off, websites like Eventbrite and Meetup, where you can create public events or join other people's events, are great if you are getting started. After all, not everyone has extroverted tendencies.
I don't believe in the whole 'introverted people cannot network' idea.

I believe that many people use introversion as an excuse not to put themselves out there. It's about where you get your energy.

As an extrovert, you would find yourself more easily adaptable to the significant events with the flashing lights and crowds. As an introvert, you would very much prefer smaller groups of people, preferably many that you already know.

There are no right or wrong ways to do it, but I've found that the so-called 'introverted' method to be more effective at building long term and beneficial relationships.

Potential mentors, prosperous businessmen, and "VIPs" would likely opt for the smaller gatherings. They are tired of navigating noisy environments where people can't talk, much less get to know each other.

They've been to enough events to know that real relationships don't involve rapid-fire rounds of "speed dating."

Speed dating is where people: rush around the room looking for targets, asking people what they do, running their pitch, handing out their name card, and vanish into thin air.

Only to repeat the process on the next unsuspecting victim. Tells you a lot about the state of regular networking events and the people who attend them.

Not all of them are as bad as I paint it, though. Chamber of Commerce events, as well as industry-related events, are still high quality.

If you want to get over the fear of meeting strangers and feel good doing so, start with small friend gatherings. Call together a few of your friends and ask them to invite one of their good friends along.

The great thing is that all attendees have been pre-vetted by the host and it would be easy to facilitate and manage those relationships

Community Leader

Several limiting beliefs surround the idea of becoming a community leader. Most would not think of themselves as a community leader, especially if they are an underdog.

The most common objection is, "Who am I to be a leader?"

Or

"I am not worthy of leading this group or organization."

Both stem from the same thing: the feeling of unworthiness. Being a community leader is working towards something greater than yourself.

It's less about yourself and more about the realization of an idea through the collective consciousness.

It's something that will bring you closer to self-actualization: the realization of your purpose, the fruition of your ideas, and the manifestation of your inert talents.

At the dissolution of your ego, your real gifts will light the world. It will bathe the globe with a purity of purpose.

The question therefore, isn't, "Who am I to be a creator, curator, leader?"

It is, "Who am I not to?"

Being a leader is an everyday decision, whether you choose to be one or not.

If you look around, communities are everywhere: your family, your workplace, your neighborhood, your company, as well as social groups. Before leading a large organization, seek to lead your pre-existing communities.

Take the first step by organizing an event, picking people together. Become a curator, facilitating interaction between people. It's the thing that is missing in the modern-day status quo, with the inception of mobile phones.

Countless opportunities could materialize as a result of you being a community leader. Not only do people see you as an authority figure, your status, credibility, and reliability also increase.

Situational Awareness

Situational awareness and adaptability are probably one of the most important things you'll ever learn. As humans, namely mammals, we need to adapt to our environments to make them work in our favor.

You might want to "be yourself" and walk into the room without any idea what you are doing.

If you do that, you risk turning people off before they have a chance to be acquainted. At times, you might even piss people off.

One time during one of my golf society's regular events, a man showed up to the driving range, not looking to play golf at all.

Instead, he went to talk to the girls and share about salsa and tried to persuade them to go to attend salsa classes with him.

It was inappropriate as he was disturbing some of the guests, who were trying to play golf. To make matters worse, some of the guests wanted to brush him off politely, but he didn't get the clue!

We had to ban him from all future events from that day forth.

If you can walk into virtually any room and adapt to the atmosphere and the people there, you are steps away from being a master communicator.

You could adjust everything you say and do to engage, connect, inspire, persuade, and sell the people you meet more effectively.

The reality is that most people lack this situational awareness, and I'll say men have the hardest time — especially those on the analytical side.

They may be analytical with their work and other areas of their life, but what I see usually happen is that they are almost clueless as to what is going on when they are out and about.

Realization comes from intuition, which comes from continued exposure to a particular stimulus.

That repeated exposure will train your subconscious mind to pick up on hidden clues. At the end of the day, if you want to gain an unfair advantage over your peers, over your competitors, you need to see what they cannot see.

I had a mentor that once told me, "Gilbert, talent is hitting targets that other people cannot hit. Genius is hitting targets other people cannot see. Thereby, innovation and progress rely on those that hit targets unseen by the masses."

Overall, situational awareness is something you get good at, or it will run you over like a train at some point in your life. Given a choice, you might as well get good at it.

Another way to increase your situational awareness is to pay close attention to what is going around you in everyday contexts. I guarantee you are going to catch things that you've probably not paid attention to before.

It's going to help you discover life in a whole new way.

For example, you could be walking down the street one day, and all of a sudden, you're picking up on the different accents of the people that are talking. The simple act of being able to distinguish someone's accent could help you instantly connect with them.

Chapter 15:
Content vs. Context

One time I was at the Park Hyatt Hotel in Tokyo, a famous hotel that was in the movie "Lost In Translation."

I've never seen or even heard of that movie until I had visited the hotel. On the way out of the hotel, I stepped into the elevator with two other gentlemen speaking with a French accent.

They were talking about the reference of the hotel to the movie, yet they haven't seen it either. So instantly, I quipped in and said, "Seems like most of us here are here because of the movie."

To which one of the gentlemen responded with, "Yes, exactly!"

"You're from France, I presume?"

"Correct, I'm from Lyon, and my friend is from Paris."

"Ahh Lyon, one of my previous co-workers, told me great things about Lyon. She attended the University of Lyon."

"Wow is that so, small world. Indeed Lyon is a great city, have you been?"

"I haven't yet, but it sounds like I should make plans now since I've made a new friend from there."

Did you notice how all of that happened?

First, it was the situational awareness that led me to the assumption that they heard about the hotel from the movie. The French accent led me to believe they are very likely from France, Canada, or Belgium.

France was more likely as the accent was a lot stronger; therefore, my guess paid off.

All of the information that I had gathered in such a short time was the underlying context behind crafting a suitable opening line.

Context, which we will talk about shortly, is critical in being able to understand not just what was said, but why.

Context is crucial to accomplishing three main objectives: relation, connection, and persuasion.

If you can understand the underlying context of an environment, you can use it to your advantage.

When I was 18, I had my first brush with real-life context.

I was studying my first year at university and was obsessed with looking for "startup" opportunities. School seemed very dull in comparison.

Up to that point, I had become pretty good friends with my computer science professor Dr. Wu.

He had been working on a High-Frequency Trading (HFT) software for the last five years. It traded stocks and equities on the stock market on autopilot at lightning-fast speeds. The software makes money from the difference between the buy and sell prices.

Dr. Wu had a problem, though. He wanted to get capital into the software, and so far, he had been using his own. The software was starting to prove its worth, so he figured it would be an excellent time to go to market.

Then there was me — an engineering student. I knew nothing about marketing and sales, but I was eager to help him. It was then my first joint venture started in my university professor's office over coffee.

Looking back, those were exciting times.

My job was to find investors willing to put money into the project. Therefore I started to look up potential events where my prospects might hang out.

My target audience was fund managers that managed millions of their client's money. Before you know it, I'm on the 7th floor of the W Hotel in Times Square, New York.

I had on a suit that was two sizes too big for me — a beer in my hand. I was three years away from the legal drinking age.

I started to walk around the room and make awkward conversations with strangers. To my surprise, some of the fund managers expressed interest in the software and asked to meet with me privately.

These were guys in their 40s and 50s talking to this kid trying to pitch them a multi-million dollar software.

It was completely unreal.

I barely knew anything about the software; I didn't have a university degree. Hell, I wasn't even old enough to drink.

I later learned that it didn't matter. You could be a nobody.

The environment created a context for me to sell. Being at that event meant I was at least someone.

Surprising as it may be, but it's entirely true.

Ever go to an event, meet someone, and think, "Wow, this person is awesome."

Then you get to know them a little longer, and you get a different feeling about them. That person is no longer as 'awesome' as you thought they were.

That is because the context of the event may have elevated their status (as well as yours) momentarily.

We make automatic snap judgments. The feeling you get with a person at a charity ball would be different than if you met them on the basketball court.

When you change the context, you change the feeling.

Speed Reading Context

Sometimes you only have a matter of seconds to figure out the context of a situation. Therefore you need to figure out how to decipher the context quickly.

Here is a method that you can employ the next time you are out and about.

Pay attention to what they are wearing. Is the person in more formal or less formal attire? Do they stick to conservative colors like blue, black, and white, or do they wear colors like red, green, yellow? Do they have any accessories?

Watch, bracelets, rings? Pay attention to other details of their belongings, do they carry an expensive backpack, suitcase, purse or are they more layback with a regular computer backpack? All of these little things will give you an initial sense of what kind of person they are.

As you may guess, someone dressed more conservatively, wearing a beautiful watch and expensive briefcase, is usually a salesperson or an executive.

Someone that is dressed less formally with a variety of colors is probably more likely to be in the creative field.

The environment you meet them in also matters.

If you see example #1 at rush hour on the train station would give you a different vibe than if you saw them in the lobby of an expensive hotel. In the former, they are probably on their way to meet someone and likely a salesperson, whereas, in the latter, it is perhaps an executive waiting for their meeting to start.

All of these little details matter, and you will have to rely on your judgment to see the differences. Speed reading context takes a bit of time to get good at, but once you have it down pat, you're good to go.

One time I was at a Starbucks at the airport and waiting in line for coffee.

The person in front of me happened to be wearing a backpack with the red letters TED on it.

Most people would instantly recognize TED as an international organization, where world-class experts give an 18-minute speech viewed globally.

There are two very likely possibilities: either he was one of the attendees or one of the speakers. There could also be other remote possibilities, such as someone giving him the backpack as a gift.

The best assumption to make here is the one that would elevate the other person as much as possible, which is the assumption that he was a speaker.

So I started the conversation by asking, "Hi there. I like your backpack, have you spoken at TED?"

He responded with," How did you know?!." It turns out he was a speaker a couple of years back.

Goes to show how well these quick inferences can make on helping you connect with people instantly.

All of this can happen in a matter of seconds. It's just whether you are willing to take a small risk.

How to Use Context: Relation

Relating with people is the first objective for discovering context. When you both share a commonality, it is easier to connect with someone instantly.

When meeting people for the first time, throw out your fishing rod and bait and see what hooks.

To have a good supply of bait, use a combination of what you observe, and what you can infer based on that.

It's almost like guessing, as you are always working with incomplete information. There's not going to be a label on people telling you exactly what kind of interests they have.

It's up to you to discover them by making statements or by asking questions.

Invariably, questions are your best bet.

When meeting someone at an event, an excellent way to find common ground is to ask, "How do you know the host?" Or "How did you find out about this event?

The answer to both of these questions will provide you with more context to then continue the conversation.

A point of relation at an event is usually the host. Since both of you may know the host, it gives you a strong commonality, which will help rapport building.

People want to know that in some ways, they feel included and that they belong.

So the need to distinguish yourself will only bring out differences that will distance you from others.

Making statements or observations may also help build rapport and relation between the two of you.

"It seems like the quality of this event is high this time."

Its a 'status elevating' statement, as you are presuming that both you and him are high-quality individuals attending the event.

However, relating to people is just one part. You don't want to stay there. That's why the next step is using context to create a connection.

How to Use Context: Connection

A connection is a line that brings everyone together. Everyone is universally connected, whether we realize it or not.

Although people come from different cultures, ethnicities, and backgrounds, we all share a similar thread.

For one, we are all homo sapiens, each with different preferences but desires, needs, wants, fears, pains, struggles, aspirations, and more.

When we see each other as different, we create distance. It is our ego tells us that we are distinct, better, superior to others. In some cases, it may be telling us the complete opposite.

All of this is a mere illusion that distracts us from really reaching out and having a genuine human touch with others.

It can be intimidating meeting people you feel has absolutely nothing in common with you.

Once you have the realization that you are no different from them at the core, just unique in perspective, you will be able to connect with them easily.

Not only do we have much to relate to, we have much to share.

Understand that every single person you encounter is going to have desires, fears, aspirations, and things they avoid.

With that in mind, you would be able to go deeper into your relationship with that person and possibly make something amazing come from it.

Your questions and your stories will act as a mirror for them to see themselves in you.

Only when that happens can you genuinely move, inspire, persuade, and sell to people.

How to Use Context: Persuasion

Look up persuasion on Amazon, and you will find thousands upon thousands of books on it.

People are fascinated with the idea of being able to get someone to do what they want.

The truth is, if you cannot learn to persuade people, you will probably have a hard time getting where you want in life.

It's like trying to run a marathon, except you are running in shallow water.

The point of all this may not be mastery for you. It may be merely finding out what you are doing that isn't serving you.

We won't get into all the scientific details of persuasion, but there is one fact we must follow.

We also share this similarity with our ancestors as well as other mammals and primates. We have a primal brain, which controls all our breathing, our organs, and all the involuntary functions in our body.

It also controls our automatic responses to events in our life. Without it, we wouldn't exist.

Most people hold natural dispositions toward specific ideas, values, and beliefs. Those thought patterns tend to stem from the primal brain as a reference to keep us 'safe.'

After all, humans used to be hunters and gatherers. Our primal brain is very much the same one as the ones of our ancestors. It keeps us alert and ready to defend ourselves from potential threats.

Therefore, when you meet someone for the first time, you will have snap judgments that define much of your relationship.

These feelings you have about the person may not even be conscious; they come from a collection of past experiences.

Perhaps that person reminds you of someone that used to bully you in middle school. It's also possible they remind you of your best friend.

You may very well not be conscious of either case, but that will profoundly impact your conversation and relationship with that person.

If you do not like them, trust them, or respect them, chances are they will not be able to persuade you no matter how hard they try.

We also have what we call our rational brain. This brain helps us process language, complex ideas, creative, and critical thinking.

We are inclined to think that we need to present a very compelling narrative to convince people. We need to use facts and figures when building our case.

What happens instead is that all new information first gets passed through the primal brain, before entering the rational mind.

Between the two brains is the area which deals with our emotions. Therefore, persuasion ultimately happens on the emotional level.

Depending on your environment, context can have a particular impact on someone's psyche and state of mind.

Physical environments are probably one of the best contexts to use subtly persuade people because it operates in the background.

Familiarity

Environments that are familiar to them may bring back positive memories and put them in a pleasant or happy state of mind.

Familiarity keeps people calm and opens them to being approached and persuaded. It can come in the form of a particular venue or the decor that contributes to creating this environment.

Novelty

Some environments are ones that they have never been to; therefore, they invoke a sort of feeling of excitement, anticipation, or perhaps anxiety.

Depending on how someone responses to new environments, it may have an impact on how likely you can persuade them.

A great way to create context is to make an observation or ask a question.

Find out which environments make them comfortable. Some settings work better because of the vibe it gives off. Are the chairs soft and warm? Is the decor pleasant? People will see you differently depending on where they meet you.

Therefore, make sure it works in your favor.

Unlocking Your Context

Either you have context for interaction, or you create it.

Your environment creates context.

As long as you have context, you can connect, become friends with, sell to, influence anyone in the world.

What's a great way to control this environment? Make people come to you. Have them come into your environment, whether through an event you are hosting, a dinner party, or a function.

You're on a long line at the airport for food. You want to talk to the person in front of or behind you. What's the context here? First, you are both waiting for the same thing. Secondly, you are both either arriving or departing to a destination.

How would you strike up a conversation here?

Here are four strategies you can implement:

1.State the obvious

"This line couldn't get any slower."

This statement works because both you and the person you are talking to share the same dilemma. There is empathy here that says, "Hey, I am like you too."

It sounds simple, but it works wonders. Sometimes people want someone that can relate to them, someone that is in the same boat as them. It might make their wait less bothersome now that someone is talking with them.

2. Ask an informed question.

"So, where are you off to today?"

Since both of you are at an airport, the person you are talking to is probably flying off somewhere.

Where you have this conversation also makes a big difference.

Another example would be at a bookstore. If you see the other person picking up a familiar book in the business section, you might ask, "I've been thinking about reading that book for a while, what got you interested in it?" Or "I read that book a while back, great book, are you usually into this genre?"

3. Make an observation

"Looks like they don't have my favorite bagel today."

Although making observations can be used to start a conversation, it depends on the situation. If there is silence on the line and all of a sudden you make random remarks, there's a good chance no one will pay attention.

If there are people already talking, then that's a different story.

4. Give a compliment

"I love your backpack, where did you get it?"

Probably one of the safest ways to strike a conversation. A compliment is a direct bridge between you and the other person.

If both of you were moving along towards your gates, you probably would have a different response than if you were waiting for something.

It's all about the context, context, context.

Mastering context and crafting your message as such will help you create opportunities where there may be none otherwise.

Crafting the Content

Your words are the content; your environment is the context.

No matter who the other person is. They have the same emotions, needs, pains as we all do.

Pedestals only exist in our minds. Successful people are just like us. Human. Flesh, blood, and bone.

You can translate this to your digital messages, as well. It doesn't need to be in person.

Again, content is the words you use in the context, which is your environment.

To say it is "exhausting" while inside an office will give a very different picture than if someone was outside in the sun and said it was "exhausting."

The same words, emotions, and feelings can be communicated in two different places and have two completely different meanings.

That's why it's so important to get this right.

Don't just pay attention to the things that people say. Pay attention to where, when as well as who said it.

Unlimited Potential

Now you are aware of context and the role it plays in our lives. People exposed to the same groups of people could play out very differently.

One may be able to create massive opportunities and results in their life while another may be struggling to get by.

Although your network and circle are essential, they are not the core principle behind getting opportunities.

There is infinite potential out in the world, at all times.

Take a walk in a crowded intersection, mall, train station. All the countless people passing you by are potential opportunities for you.

The challenge is figuring out to capture value out of those potential opportunities. Chances are, most people don't.

They just let opportunities pass by and don't even see one when it presents itself.

They say that success is when opportunity meets preparation. You can prepare all you want, but if an opportunity is right under your nose and you can't see it, then what's the use?

Chapter 16:
Gaining An Unfair Advantage

An unfair advantage. We all want one, but not everyone gets one.

Some were born with it or came from prestige and nobility. The chances are that it's not you.

For most of us, either we were raised in middle-class families or down that spectrum.

Life, at times, was rough. We saw those that had what we didn't, and we felt that difference first hand.

I remember, at one point, my family was living off food stamps.

We couldn't afford new clothes, so instead, I got hand-me-downs donated from others.

At the time, I accepted my situation as my reality.

In the 4th grade, I recall that some of those second-hand clothes didn't fit me that well.

I came to school some days dressed like a girl.

The edge of my t-shirt touched my shoulder, and my shorts were so short that my underwear was popping out when I sat down.

Kids regularly made fun of me because of what I wore.

That was a particularly traumatic experience for me. Being bullied was the norm.

An unfair advantage didn't exist for me then. It wasn't until I wandered into one of the most prestigious clubs in Hong Kong and saw the difference between the haves and have nots.

Those that were in the upper echelon of wealth were mingling amongst each other. Heads of state, listed company chairpersons, celebrities all rubbed shoulders in a booth discussing their horses' performance.

The "commoners" relegated to the lower stands to thumb their newspapers and guessed which horse to place their bets.

The contrast was stark and it made me wonder.

How could I get myself into that booth?

Then it dawned on me. On the one hand, I could work my way up and become someone of "importance."

By then, that probably wouldn't matter. That is because, by then, I would probably have access to most of the influential circles anyway.

That's the thing. Those with prestige will treat it as a regular occurrence, while those without would treat it like a big deal.

Ever go into a fancy hotel lobby and marvel at how beautiful it is?

Chances are, someone that frequently is a patron there wouldn't share your enthusiasm. That's because they see it as "normal."

The first way to get invited and be part of influential circles is to treat it as a regular thing. Not in a superficial or stuck up way. Just as a gesture of, "well, I've been here before." "I belong."

If you have ever tried getting into a popular nightclub on a Saturday night, you will understand how difficult it is to get in if your name isn't on the list.

However, sometimes, just acting as you belong is enough to get you in.
Same with these circles that will open doors for you. Treat it as if you belong.

Learn from those that go to these events. See how they act and emulate with your style. I stress authenticity because if you try too hard, you will have the opposite desired effect.

People don't take well those that are pretentious and try too hard to fit in.

Appearing too perfect will have unintended consequences that will leave you looking unapproachable or disingenuous.

It's more of an art than a science, but there is a science behind it.

Anyone can create an unfair advantage with the right mindset, habits, and practice.

An unfair advantage nowadays is not owned by celebrities or well-known entrepreneurs, or officials, but by influencers.

Influencers, in a nutshell, are those that have an impact on a specific niche process.

Which means they have a near-absolute influence on a particular group or groups of people. They can make a statement and have it be taken for gospel almost immediately.

However, you don't NEED to be an influencer to have that sort of influence.

You can start with what you already have. The key is that you have a platform that you can begin to leverage.

It's challenging to try and join a particular circle, regardless of what kind of work you do.

All the "inner circle" groups are getting all the business, the connections, and opportunities.

It's no wonder that the rich get richer. It's always been an unfair game. The point is not to change the rules, but to change how you operate within them.

How to Get An Unfair Advantage?

You have a choice. Not everyone will become an influencer.

Some will try. Most will fail. That is not to say don't try, but there is a better way. It comes from first improving your base and foundation.

You need to have a core set of skills through which people know and respect you.

What's it in for them?
The mindset shift that changed it all for me was going from "what's it in for me" to "what's it in for them."

Everyone you meet will invariably be thinking in their interests. Therefore, by putting yourself first, you don't stand a chance to get the proper attention you require.

Instead, if you place yourself in their shoes and think of how you can help them, you open up a gateway for you to help them.

It goes from, "how can I benefit from them to "how can they benefit from me."

I used to walk into the room, thinking, "how much money could I make from the people here?"

Now I focus my effort on helping at least five people every day.

That has been the small change that has made the most substantial difference in my life.

Questions To Ask

What are the questions you must first ask yourself before you start trying to gain an unfair advantage?

1. What is your ultimate goal?

What do you genuinely want to accomplish in your life? This includes not only your career goals but also your personal and spiritual goals.

2. What is your definition of success for achieving your goal?

Achieving your goal isn't based on other people's definitions of success. That is because everyone has different reasons for doing something and a different starting point.

For someone that grew up in poverty, getting out of debt is already a success. For someone that has all the basic needs taken care of, success may involve becoming a business owner, or an executive at a reputable company.

Then for someone who was born into wealth, success may mean something completely different.

There is no right or wrong answer to this question, only that it is an answer arrived at by your own devices.

Take as much time as you need to sit with the answers to these questions. They usually aren't answers that come naturally.

Quite often, we suppress the need to answer them because they are difficult. The questions require us to confront ourselves. Maybe what we thought to be correct or valid no longer applies to us.

That means we need to admit that a previous version of our thinking is no longer serving us. It hurts, but it must happen to get us to a place that brings us lasting peace, joy, and happiness.

The worst thing might be getting everything you thought would bring you happiness only to be surprised that it doesn't.

3. What are the critical milestones of achieving your goal?

By breaking your ultimate goal into smaller pieces, you make grand goals seem a lot closer to reality. Sometimes we procrastinate because a goal seems too large, too big for us to even know where to start.

4. What are the winning conditions for each of these milestones?

Back to using winning conditions to define when you know you have completed a milestone.

Getting 10,000 users for your online platform isn't the same as getting 10,000 engaged users, and isn't the same as getting 10,000 paying customers.

It's easy to set a number and cheat our way into hitting a target, whether by natural or unnatural means.

5. What are the strengths that will help you achieve your goals?

Understanding what you are good at goes a long way. It is silly to think you are going to be in the NBA if you are in your twenties and 5 '5'.

Brutal honesty is the best policy. There's no need to kid yourself by proclaiming goals that aren't in alignment with your strengths.

For sure, there are many goals you can accomplish without having every strength required.

Strengths will make your life a lot easier. It highlights what you can get even better at.

6. What are your weaknesses?

Often we go trying to fix or hide our weaknesses. As if it is something to be ashamed of.

Every person that has ever walked this Earth has a form of weakness. Sometimes weaknesses are easier to spot than others.

For example, I was born with my hips angled inwards. It has led me to walk with an awkward inward step, something that I have hated.

I dread running. The reason is because of my condition, my joints strain easily, and I can't run for long without getting completely exhausted.

At the same time, I've come to accept that it is part of me.

If I can't change it, then I might as well get over it.

The question is, what is something you know about yourself that you haven't yet gotten over?

Something that is dis-empowering you because you are spending so much effort trying to suppress it.

7. Who can help us get closer to achieving these goals? Who are the people that need to get involved?

Knowing exactly the kind of people that need to get on board with your journey is essential for us to get where we want to go.

Thinking we can do it alone is just a recipe for disaster. It's time to put down the ego and look into the people in your network and people outside it that can help you.

They could be mentors, early clients, key partners, sponsors, anyone with significance that can help you move the needle.

More importantly, it is people that can help you compliment your weaknesses.

Make a mini list of people that immediately come to mind. It doesn't have to be an elaborate list, just one that has people that you believe will be helpful to help you realize your goals.

Later on, you will be making a much longer list with a more systematic approach.

8. What is your timeline?

Note this is not a deadline. Timelines can be adjusted, deadlines not so much.

The reason for adding this sort of flexibility is to allow for changes to occur. I used to put a fixed deadline on my goals. When it seemed that I was not going to achieve my goal, what ended up happening was I started getting lazy.

These are the questions you need to get clear on before moving on.

There will be a lot of tactics and strategies in this book that you can employ, but none of them matter if you are not clear on what you are trying to achieve.

That said, gaining an unfair advantage doesn't have to be esoteric or something reserved for the few.

Never have we been in a time where human connection is required by most, but created by so few. If you can learn how to navigate the trenches with people, to empower them, inspire them, then you will ultimately be able to achieve anything that you want.

Creating communities

The Weaken Bonds of Connection
Community plays a huge role in this book. It is the thread that weaves people together.

Since introducing the internet, mobile phones, and social media, people have connected with those from all over the world. At the same time, it has made us distant from each other.

There was a time where we would have long conversations over food. Nowadays, almost everyone is on their phone during dinner.

It's hard to be present with so many distractions. It's even harder to be present with people. It requires a conscious effort.

Social awkwardness has become an enormous problem. As people's phones are conditioning them, it makes it hard for them to connect with other people.

Micro and niche communities are going to play a massive role in society in the coming decade.

Physical meetings, offline events are going to be more crucial than ever before. Online communities got us the connectivity that we desire, but offline communities allow for deep connections to form.

That's where you come in. One of the most powerful things you can do in the coming few years is to position yourself as a leader of an organization.

One of my first mentors shared with me something that I'll never forget. He is the Founder Emeritus and Ex-Chairman of a global shipping company.

I was in his office one day, and I could already smell the aroma of the tea he was brewing.

He is a big fan of the traditional tea ceremony where you have a unique table where you place tea leaves into a stone pot and slowly watch it boil.

At one point, he said, "Positions can be given and taken. A founder, however, isn't a position. It's an identity that will stay with you forever."

I found that statement to be profound. Being a founder, co-founder of an organization is more than a position. It signifies that you've created something special.

No one can ever take that away from you. A title like CEO could easily be stripped and taken away.

To be a founder of a community presents a lot of challenges, but also a lot of opportunities.

When you create the environment, you create the context to connect with anyone that comes inside your community.

A good example is my golf society. I am the organizer, the president, the facilitator. When people want to attend my events, I am the center of influence. People come to me. I create the basis for a connection to happen.

My golf society, in this case, is my platform. Everyone has a choice of platform. Maybe you have a reasonable following on social media, a blog, a Youtube channel, a podcast. Or none of those.

The idea is to create a platform for yourself to bring people to you.

Back in 2012, I had just learned to play golf. In Hong Kong, I found there were very few groups that I could join that were similar to myself. Pretty much all the groups were for retired folks.

What I decided to do was to start a group on meetup.com so that I could find people that were a similar age to me to play golf with.

It all started on the evening of August 21st, 2012, on a driving range, the first event I've ever held for the group.

I remembered only two people showed up. Not a big deal, we just went and played golf.

A few problematic months went by. I was on the verge of throwing in the towel. There were nights where no one would show up.

I kept telling myself, "Well, no problem. I'll just play golf."

Then in October that year, it all changed. I met my 2nd co-founder, Ray, who was also an enthusiastic golfer. He happened to find my group on Meetup as well.

He was delighted to find the group as he also had trouble finding people to play golf with.

The rest was history. We started to work together to make the group grow and noticed our events began to get much more significant.

Later on, we had a 3rd co-founder that came on board, and once again, that accelerated our growth.

It started as a recreation group, but only one short year later, we changed the nature of the group to a golf society. Not only was it a golf society, but membership was by invitation only.

it meant that if people would like to be a member, the Board would have to send a formal invitation to them.

A few years in, we decided to form a Board, which would determine the day to day operations of our community. We also formed four different committees to govern our events, members, and more.

Every year we had three major tournaments, golf-related events each month, an annual dinner, and a Christmas party.

As I write this, last week was our society's 7th-anniversary dinner. It amazes me how incredible everything has been for the community. We have built something that many high-quality people congregate, meet through, and bond over.

Many of our members are well-to-do professionals and business owners, and it all started with an idea, an event.

That is not the only platform that I have to stand on. I also launched a podcast in September 2018 called the Live Your Edge Podcast. It was where I interviewed people continually pushing their boundaries and doing great things as business owners, entrepreneurs, and digital nomads.

Once again, I started by interviewing my friends who had reasonably sound businesses. As time went on, I was able to talk to a lot of the more influential people like John Lee Dumas, a 7-figure podcaster, Neil Patel,

a well-known SEO guy, and David Meltzer, a notable social media influencer.
It all started bit by bit, a staircase that was building the steps as it went along.

That's how all platforms get built; you place a higher block with each new step.

Finally, my other platforms include my social media following. Something that I've spent a lot of time building. I realized that although many people build reasonable audiences, social media as a foundation is quite shaky.

Communities that have a physical, as well as digital presence, is a lot more reliable.

My three platforms are my golf society, my social media following, and my podcast. Depending on the person I want to meet, I will use a different platform.

If I meet someone that plays golf, I will use that as a basis for connection and value add. If it is someone influential, I might use a podcast.

You don't need to start a podcast or a community. These are all examples. There are many different platforms out there.

Even an alumni group can be a platform if you have any leadership positions in an organization or community, or church.

You want people to come to you where you are. That's what gives you power. Here are some of the strategies you can employ to start building up your foundation.

Ladder Principle

The Ladder Principle is one of my favorite principles when it comes to meeting new people.

Now what is the ladder principle? It is leveraging social proof and taking what you already have as leverage to get what you want.

Let me give you an example. Recently I was able to interview influencers with hundreds of thousands and even a million followers. It didn't happen all at once but in stages.

When I mapped out the people I wanted to reach, I separated them by tiers. Tier 1 people were the super well-known influencers that were difficult to reach. Conversely, Tier 3 was less known and more comfortable to approach.

I started getting Tier 3 people on my podcast, then using 3 of those names to pitch Tier 2 people. Then once I got a few Tier 2 people on the show, I used those names to get Tier 1 people on the show.

The same applies to clients. Tier 1 might be an ultra-high net worth individual. Whereas Tier 2 and 3 may just be Newly high net worth individuals.

By working your way up the ladder and using the previous step as leverage, you open many doors that otherwise wouldn't be open.

You can apply the ladder principle to almost every part of your life.

If you want to improve in a particular skill, you can use the ladder principle to build your skillset by adding rugs on a ladder.

Instead of trying to go for mastery instantly, take big leaps.

The key to using this for skills is first identifying the different rugs on the ladder required for mastery.

Then you would take these ladder rungs apart and break them into smaller, more manageable chunks.

Then focus your effort on mastering these small chunks one at a time.

You will find it has an enormous impact on your ability to improve in a short time.

Let's take the skill of copywriting, for example. To use the ladder principle with this skill, you will first identify the core components of a good copy.

First, there is an attention grabber. Then you have things like storytelling, use of persuasive words, and more.

Break down the attention grabber into smaller pieces: the headline, subtitles, power words, etc.

By performing this action, you will get a better idea of what is going on and not spend years stuck at the same plateau.

It will allow you to see your strengths and weaknesses. Ask yourself how you might amplify those strengths and minimize the weaknesses.

If you take away nothing in this book at all except this principle, that would already be enough. That is because the ladder principle will help you reach success faster than ever before.

Top to Bottom Introductions

It is far easier to get introductions to high-quality individuals when you start at the top than at the bottom.

You may feel that people at the top don't have the time to help others. That could not be further from the truth.

There are generally two camps of people.

One camp believes that you need to become successful so that you can help people.

Then there is the other camp, which believes that people are successful because they help others.

In my experience, those that have mentored me, guided me, worked with me, and helped me on my journey has been more than generous when it comes to giving.

It's normal to see those that aren't quite there yet being a lot more guarded with their time. There's a lot more 'what's in it for me?' going on in their mind.

On the flip side, those that have achieved great success in life may be focusing on making themselves useful to others.

Sure there is a caveat. *Successful people are guarded with their time until you can show that you aren't going to waste it.*

It's crazy that there are people that would ask for advice and chose to do absolutely nothing with it. Especially those that get advice for free.

Therefore, at times, it makes sense paying a potential mentor, not because they need your money, but because it shows that you are putting skin in the game.

In short, you have something to lose from not taking action.

Successful people tend to have a well-established network of trusted parties and would be more than happy to put you in touch with relevant individuals given you have earned their trust.

Trust will be transferred over to their contact, which will make contacting big names a whole lot easier than trying to work your way up.

It may seem a bit counter-intuitive to the ladder principle, but it isn't.

While the ladder principle is about working your way up by breaking down influencers and hard to reach people by tiers, defined by the macro overview, top to bottom is the micro view, where you do the actual approaching.

It can be hard at first to hold both concepts in your mind, as they seem to be contradicting each other.

Top to bottom is about reaching out to that hard to reach individual, whether in Tier 1, Tier 2, Tier 3 of your plan, but keeping in mind the gradual.

It means adding value to the VIP. It means showing that you are not there to waste time but looking to create value for others. It includes making good with their gatekeeper, which can be a challenge at times.

Understanding Gatekeepers and How To Communicate With Them

Gatekeepers can be a challenge if you allow it to be.

You see, the gatekeeper is there to serve as a barrier between you and their boss. They need to ensure that they don't waste their time.

Therefore, they serve as a necessary filter to ensure that people looking to waste time are effectively blocked, while those that provide value to their boss to be allowed in.

Gatekeepers have been around since the beginning when there were monarchs and royalty.

They are someone that holds the keys to getting in touch and establishing contact with their employer.

They are to be treated like VIPs because they are one. They hold power to modify their employer's calendar, among other things. They can shut you out from their boss before you even have a chance to get in touch. They hold the keys to the kingdom.

And they can sometimes be mistreated by other people that come into contact with them. It may be easy to dismiss them, but that is a huge mistake.

Those that try to overstep them in efforts to get to their boss may soon find themselves shun or blocked from even reaching out.

Don't underestimate their power because the power they wield in an organization is enormous. They should be treated like every other human, with respect and dignity, and also as a VIP that gets things done.
Here is a simple checklist for you.

1. Ask for the gatekeeper's name.

It applies especially when you call a VIP's office, and the call gets routed to the secretary or executive assistant. The first thing is to figure out how to address them.

Try, "How may I address you?"

If you skip this step, there's a good chance that you won't start the relationship right. Best not to overlook the small details.

2. Use the gatekeeper's name immediately.

This shows that you care and also as a way for you to remember their name.

3. Thank the gatekeeper for the opportunity

Note that they don't work for you, and don't need to do anything for you. Anything the gatekeeper does is out of their own free will.
Here's a fun fact.

They probably know more about their boss than anyone else. They interact with them virtually every single day and know their contact base by heart.

A gatekeeper probably knows more about their work and personal life than perhaps their spouse.

They have access to information that pretty much no one else is aware of, and they are trusted to safeguard it.

Now that you know more about gatekeepers and their importance to get in front of an influential person. How do you converse and build a relationship with them?

4. Understand the gatekeeper's objective

Although they might sound intimidating, they are just doing their job.

Their job is to keep out unwanted pests. These include people trying to waste their bosses' time, advertisers, scam calls, and so forth.

There's a second half to this. Although they want to filter out the pests, they also want to attract good people into the company of the boss.

It might come in the form of opportunities or people with genuine intentions that respect their authority.

5. Be brief with what you want

You should make sure you let the gatekeeper know what you want, but you should also include statements of high value that help you stand out from other people, even reaching out.

Mention where you have heard of or previously interacted with their boss. State your reason, are you trying to get on the phone with them?

Are you offering them an opportunity? Are you looking for a chance to meet with them in person?

Share as much as you can in a few short sentences, and allow the gatekeeper to filter your request accordingly.

What I've found to work is transparency.

Sometimes you have nothing tangible to offer. Just say so.

Tell them; I have nothing to offer your boss at this time being. I have been following their content for a while; I just have a few questions that I'd like to ask them. Won't take more than a few minutes.

That would work better than trying to make up an excuse to get rid of the gatekeeper.

People try that all the time. They make up reasons, such as "I have something vital to talk to him or her about" Or "I have a personal matter to discuss with so and so."

I used to be a gatekeeper at one of my previous jobs. Since I worked in sales, I was in the front line, and that meant some of the calls going into the office went my way.

On occasion, I would be on the receiving end of people with a nasty attitude and treated me like an obstacle rather than a person. It's one of the worst feelings ever.

Some people might have gotten through to my boss if they were just a little bit more polite and real with their intentions, instead of saying,

"Please connect me with Rob; it's a personal matter."

When I ask a little bit further, the person on the line says, "I told you it's a personal matter, now connect me."

It can be a very straightforward process if you let it be. By combining your understanding of the gatekeeper, their role in serving their boss, and communicating with them in a way where it is easy for them to forward your call to their boss, you are one step closer to befriending and building relationships with the influential.

It's a skill that takes time to hone and achieve mastery. I do not claim to master this skill myself; it is something that is an ongoing process because every company is different. Every gatekeeper is different.

They come in different forms. They may not be the direct secretary of the boss. It could be the receptionist; it could be their spouse, you get the idea.

Gatekeepers come in all shapes of forms, and if you ever get confused, just treat everyone you meet with the same level of respect and grace because you never know.

Reverse Selling

Reverse selling is a sales technique I've created over the years after being sick of just pushing ideas and products onto people.

Instead, I learned to get people to sell themselves on working with me.

Reverse selling is essentially getting your customers to sell you on buying your products and services. Instead of you constantly straining to drive the sale forward, you are instead creating an environment where the customer can convince themselves to own your product. Best of all, it becomes their idea to purchase from you.

It may seem odd that a customer would ever want to sell you on buying your products, but it happens every day. Think about an exclusive club or organization such as EO (Entrepreneur Organization) or a prestigious country club.

They are perfect examples where the customers, new and prospective members, sell the club on granting them its membership.
Money is not enough to become a member of EO; often, the customers need to justify their qualifications through other means.

Realize that customers make a majority of purchases based on status, or perceived status. If you could paint a picture of increasing their status by owning the product or service, they are much more likely to take action.

Usually, we often focus on highlighting the features, advantages, and benefits of what we sell. Still, we must understand the key drivers behind the customer to make the sale.

By having this idea of status elevation in mind, you will be able to own and utilize the power of reverse selling.

It's by no means a 'new sales methodology,' nor does it claim to be one. Reverse selling is a powerful tool to add to your repertoire that you can apply to get your sales skills to the next level.

It comes from the ability to observe what's happening and calibrate or adapt to make someone's life easier. You want to put the prospect in the driver's seat, as if they are moving the conversation forward.

Here are 3 core steps to achieve that. I use the acronym O.A.R to highlight these three steps. Think of it as an OAR in a boat that helps you paddle your way to your destination.

1. Step 1: O is for Observing what their immediate needs are by what the other person is sharing with you. To encourage them to share, ask them about their experiences or stories.
2. Step 2: A is for Asking Questions to allow them the space to elaborate and go deeper into those stories and issues.
3. Step 3: R is for Reflecting or mirror what they say back to them to encourage even more sharing from them.

Once you get them talking, it can get very tempting to share your own opinions! Don't!

Just ask the questions and shut up! Let them talk. If you do most of the talking, they are going to get bored out of their minds.

People love talking about themselves. Think about it. Their friend circle consists of other like-minded individuals who all have their issues, challenges, and stories.

Only a small fraction of what they are thinking about gets shared. Everything else gets drowned out by everyone else's stories.

By acting as the soundboard, you are providing them with a rare opportunity to vent. It's a fantastic feeling. The belief that someone is willing to lend an ear and provide undivided attention towards them.

Here's the juicy part of it all.

When I was managing a community of my own, we had a policy where we screen and invite prospective members to be part of the community.

We also had to frame the situation in a way where they were trying to pitch us on why they would be eligible to be a member.

Flipping the script makes this technique so powerful. Groucho Marx famously said, "I don't wish to be part of any club that would have me as a member."

My interpretation is that the prospect needs a robust and compelling reason to be part of the club then the club itself. And this statement embodies the spirit of reverse selling at its core.

It works because they are doing the selling, making the reasons, and justifying why they should make the purchase.

When you say it, they are skeptical, but when they say it, they believe it to be true.

So the idea is to get them to highlight the benefits and how it will serve their life and justify the drawbacks that they would get from investing in your product or service.

If you aren't in sales or don't own a business, that's completely fine.

Once again, everyone is in the game of sales. Imagine applying this for your interactions with people you are trying to persuade. Visualize how different the outcome might be as opposed to trying to shove ideas down each other's throat.

By having the other person validate their claims, it came from them and is more likely to stick. No one wants to admit they were wrong.

Just make them right and right about ideas that you want them to embrace.

In the movie Inception, the protagonist, played by Leonardo DiCaprio, is a thief that specializes in stealing secrets from people's dreams and subconscious. Later on, he's on a mission to plant seeds in the mind of the heir of an energy company, in a bid to try and convince him to dissolve the company.

The point is to make the target believe that it was their idea all along to do what you want them to do. Whether it is to buy your product or take a particular course of action.

It is subtle yet effective. Remember to use all of these techniques in this book responsibly. It is not to mislead or manipulate people into believing things that aren't true.

Hold your moral compass at heart, for it is the only thing that separates us from the conman and scammers who only seek personal gain while sacrificing everything else.

By using these techniques, you will be one step further down the road for mastering the art of influence and persuasion.

Chapter 17:
Success Habits

As Aristotle famously put it, "Excellence is merely the practice of everyday habits.

These everyday habits form who we are. Yet most of the time, people live their lives on autopilot. They don't have set practices, therefore they are defined by them.

Some habits serve you, while some don't. The purpose is not to have all the best practices in the world.

Habits exist so that your day works for you, not happens to you. In the absence of habits, you would go about your day without a

clear structure, ultimately affecting your productivity, effectiveness, motivation, and mental well-being.

It would be near impossible to keep up the routine, especially if you have ten things to do before breakfast.

It's about stripping away what doesn't work for you and replacing it with something that does.

I've spent years trying to figure out powerful habits, and each time I have to go back to the drawing board to modify them.

With time, I've come to realize that as underdogs, what we seek is an improvement. As long as we improve and get better, we can accept virtually anything life throws at us.

What gets measured gets accomplished.

So as long as there is progress, we will continue onwards. Otherwise, we may falter, lose hope, and give up.

Even as I write this book, I've made a habit of writing every morning and writing down how many words and pages I've made progress on every day.

It has helped me stay on track as well as accelerate my progress.

Your daily habits towards your goals may be different, but the principles are the same.

They need to be bite-sized and easily doable. It doesn't take a lot of individual effort or brainpower. Things that are easy to do are also easy not to do.

At the same time, those habits need to contribute to a bigger picture, the purpose of instilling the practice in the first place.

One of the habits that people try so hard to commit to but ultimately fail to do is waking up at a particular time.

There are many experts out there telling you to wake up before 6 am, 5 am, and some even say you need to wake up at 4 am.

If you blindly follow their advice without really asking yourself why you need to be up at that time, you're not going to be able to maintain that habit for long.

The same goes for any other habit out there.

There are a few universal habits that have made a positive impact on my life, which keeps coming up over and over.

It is not a complete set of habits that you could do, but more as a guide and reference to the patterns that shaped my life. Pick the ones that you want to start with and do it.

Making Your Bed

This habit is crucial. The purpose of this habit is to complete your first small but personal task of the day. It creates momentum for you to do all the other tasks of the day. Also, it looks good to come back home to a bed already made.

No matter where I am staying, whether at home, a hotel, or an Airbnb, I will make my bed every morning. Period.

Saves the cleaning staff some effort to make the room, but also gives me a sense of control of my day. Not everything you do is entirely in your control, but making your bed is one of them.

For some high performers, this is known as the domino effect. One practice sets other habits into motion.

Meditation Practice

Mediation is a form of mindfulness practice. It's usually associated with sitting still but can be done even amid noisy distracting environments.

The purpose of meditation is to clear your mind, to create a space where you can respond to daily stimulus, rather than react to it. The silence at first is hard to cope with; we are used to thinking thousands of thoughts. Once you get used to the practice, it becomes easier to get into a meditative state.

Every morning I would do a minimum of 10 minutes of meditation. Although everyone you speak with will recommend a different duration, after years of meditating, I default to 10 minutes.

I'm aware that some recommend as long as 1-hour mediations, and I admit, I feel different when I meditate for one hour.

Most people won't go there, however. If you can control an entire hour of silence, you can reclaim the remaining 23 hours of the day.

See it as a productivity boost for the rest of the day. At the same time, with so much going on around us, meditation has never been more critical.

It gives us a grand perspective on viewing things that happen; it allows us to create enough distance to see the event more objectively.

Seeing the full truth may be very well out of our reach, but we can get as close as possible to it when our minds are in a state of calm.

We can react to things that happen, or we can respond to them. The ability to respond is the logos behind responsibility.

Start somewhere quiet and sit with your legs crossed. Rest the back of your palms on your knees. The reason for having the palms up is that the inside of your hand is more sensitive and can cause distractions.

Now close your eyes and breathe in and out slowly. There is no right or wrong way to meditate, and probably a million different ways to do it.

Meditation mobile applications are quite useful when it comes to assisting your meditation practice. I typically use the app called 'Calm,' but some people prefer apps like 'Headspace.'

If you miss a day, don't worry, start all over. There is no right and wrong when it comes to mindfulness.

Bonus: Walking meditation

Walking meditation is similar to the meditation practice discussed. Instead of sitting still in a room, you would walk around, preferably in nature.

Whether you are on your way to a meeting, to work, or to get something to eat, you can practice walking meditation.

Spend your time focused on your breathing, and pay attention to each step you take as it hits the concrete.

Pay attention to the wind, or lack of one. Notice the rays of the sun touching your body, gracing it with warmth.

Often this habit alone will create a sense of peace right before you are about to perform an important task.

Whether you are calm when you perform the task or stressed is entirely in your control. This practice will help you reclaim peace in virtually any environment.

Exercise

Exercise has been instrumental in providing me with more energy to go about my day. Missing physical activity can take a considerable toll on my energy levels, simply because I haven't moved around enough.

Like with mediation, there is no right or wrong way to do it. I focus on high-intensity excretion.

Pushups, pull-ups, or anything I can get my hands on in the morning. Some people are regular gym-goers, while some haven't been in the gym for ages. Both are fine, but beyond your typical routine, morning exercise is so that you can wake up rejuvenated and ready to take on the day.

When you engage in vigorous exercise early in the morning, you allow the mind to wake up, saying, "it's time to get busy."

We often neglect our health when we go to work on other parts of our life, especially when it comes to our career.

We spend long hours in the office, grinding away, in hopes of improving our situation while neglecting our body.

Productivity from taking care of health translates into more energy for our work. It makes us more confident of ourselves, thereby improving our relations with other people we associate with on a day-to-day basis.

If you feel time-constrained with a busy schedule, I have a simple exercise routine you could follow.

5-minute morning warm-up

Spend the two minute waking up with a brisk round of jumping jacks, wherever you happen to be at the time.

Then spend the next minute doing pushups. Don't keep count of how many you do, just keep doing them until the minute is up. Make sure you have a timer going. Focus on every movement. Be present, and don't think about the next thing you are going to do.

Be with the movement. Pay attention to your inhales and exhales.
It's not about the completion of the task, but your presence. Usually, we perform things like pushups without ever noticing what is going on.

Now, after you have completed the pushups, spend the next 1-2 minutes doing jumping squats. Bend your knees as you squat down, then push down with your legs and explode into the air.

By now, you will start to feel that rush of power coursing through your veins.

It only takes 5 minutes, and you will realize that it doesn't take a whole lot of effort and certainly not any equipment.

All that is required is the habit of doing it, day in and day out no matter what.

Again, what is easy to do is also easy not to do.

If it is too much to start with, then begin with just the 1 minute of jumping jacks. After a few days, add the push ups. Finally, after a week, add the jumping squats.

Now, if you're up for a challenge, you're welcome to include your variations of the exercise.

Top 3 Tasks

After I've made at least 2 of the above three habits, I check my task and goal list.

My task list comprises of my Top 3 Tasks that I want to accomplish today, as well as 'nice to have' tasks. As long as I complete my Top 3 tasks, I will call that day a success. Too often, we place as many tasks as we can fit into a day and try to finish all of them.

There are tasks we don't need to do in the first place. Some don't get you towards your end goals, and some are simply there to fill time gaps.

It takes effort to come up with a Top 3 Task list; therefore, I suggest that you complete it the night before.

Jim Rohn said, "Don't start the day until you have finished it." Simply means that you shouldn't start your day until you have planned it the night before.

What I usually do is plan my entire week full of my Top 3 tasks on Sundays. It gives me an overview of the whole week ahead and gives me clarity rather than winging it.

The night before, I would examine my list to see if a situation requires it to be adjusted; otherwise, I will take a mental note and sleep on it.

That would allow me to wake up without having to think about what I am going to do the next day. With all that extra bandwidth, I could use it to dominate the day.

Willpower is Limited

After all, willpower is a finite resource. Every time we have to expend our brains to do complicated things like planning, it saps willpower.

We are tired both mentally and physically after a long day at work. It is most natural, then, to fall into lazy habits such as watching Netflix, Youtube, or scrolling through Instagram.

Use this to your benefit by taking care of the substantial planning before you sleep.

Eating the Frog on Steroids

Eating the frog is the habit of doing the hardest thing first thing In the morning.

The process means as a way to pick up momentum to complete other tasks later on.

I'd like to expand on that. After doing a bit of testing on my end, I realized that doing the hardest thing in the morning is excellent, but it would be awesome if you can use that opportunity to clamp down on as many tasks as you can while you are still 'hot'.

Motivation and energy rise and fall throughout the day.

Ideally, you want to finish most of your tasks for the day before lunchtime.

It may sound crazy, but when we tap into a 'flow state,' we move a lot faster. Once we overcome the friction of inaction, keeping the work workflow going is a lot easier.

You may find it is better to batch several difficult tasks in a single morning. Meaning you pick your top 3 hardest tasks and bang them all out at once. Everything else in your day will be a piece of cake.

These are some of the habits that you could start incorporating into your daily routine. Of course, don't expect to start doing all of them at once. It would be near impossible to maintain for more than a week or so.

Pick 1 or 2 that resonate with you. A habit that you feel would add a lot of benefits to your life. Then start doing that. Keep at it for at least 14-21 days before adding any new habits.

It takes about 21 days for a new habit to solidify. Sometimes that period is longer, sometimes shorter.

It is tempting to add more habits before you are ready for them. You risk screwing up all of the patterns that you've already built into your life.

Applying the Ladder Principle To Habits

You can also apply the Ladder Principle to building up your habits. When I started writing this book, I set a daily target of 500 words per day.

After the first week, I increased the daily target by 100. I would repeat this process every week. Within a month, I was writing at least 900 words per day.

It took me 30 days to add 22,000+ more words to my manuscript, which was pretty crazy for me.

Before that, I was stuck at a measly 13,000 words for an entire year while I procrastinated on my book day in, day out.

Use the ladder principle to build your habits in increments.

For example, if you are aiming to get to an hour of meditation every day, starting at 10 minutes. Every week, add 5 minutes to your daily practice.

Within ten weeks, you will have built up to a 1-hour meditation; that is if your goal is getting to an hour-long meditation.

You can also experiment with increments that increase with time. Instead of increasing the duration/ amount each week by a fixed number, you can improve it by an expanding figure after a few cycles.

That will help you improve your practice faster, but it is also more challenging.

In conclusion, the power of habit will set you free. Start with smaller habits and slowly build it up to practices that are harder to take up.

Chapter 18: Unlocking Opportunity

Finding Opportunities Around You

There are opportunities all around you. It just depends on whether you are willing to seize them.

Two people can walk into the same room and see different things. That's the difference between human subjectiveness.

One person could just see a group of people that are obstacles to his or her goal, while the other person sees them all as potential gateways to growth and opportunity.

The choice is all yours, and only you could walk the path. No one will take the first step for you.

Once a week, you should consider spending considerable time seeking opportunities. Whether that is browsing online for a job, researching people to speak to,

Syncing what you have

When we look at our life as many different unrelated parts, it will seem that way.

When we see those elements as parts of an interconnected system, everything changes. You will begin to see links between every part of your life.

Your health and fitness affect your energy levels, which affect your work productivity, your relationships with your peers, friends, as well as significant other.

When it comes to getting an unfair advantage, people typically have several reasons not to try.

1. "I need to have a strong personal brand, a solid platform, and good sales skills to be able to create opportunities in my life."

It is because of that; people keep themselves stuck by comparing themselves with others, instead of working on themselves.

They spend numerous hours trying everything that doesn't get them any closer to their goal. They are in a cycle of chasing shiny objects. Then they wonder why they don't get anywhere.

It prevents them from seeing the bigger picture. For you to get ahead of the crowd, you can't be doing what everyone else is doing.

You can't be going out on Friday nights celebrating absolutely nothing, yelling "Yolo," (a phrase coined in recent years to mean 'you only live once') and using that as an excuse to have fun. The reality is, you're sabotaging many parts of your life when you take up activities that don't help your life in any way.

The truth is that if your daily habits and goals do not align, no matter how hard you try, it will always be an uphill battle for you. It will be a game of struggle, a game you don't want to play for the sake of it.

We don't need to make things any harder for ourselves than they need to be. I also had that same problem when I first got into the workplace. I would try different projects for a few months, only to drop them when they seem like they have lost promise.

I spent hours trying looking through articles on how to improve my personal brand — spending money on flashy clothes that I didn't need.

I was trying to look like a million bucks. None of that was helping me get to a million dollars.

Sometimes it's not about getting better, especially when you are already on your way to improving and acquiring more skills.

It's about taking what you already have and making it work to your benefit.

That's what we call a SYSTEMATIC APPROACH. Systems work best when they are synchronized.
- Your pre-existing personal brand
- Your pre-existing platforms/ points of leverage
- Your pre-existing strategy for achieving your goals.

Here's an exercise that will help you take account of what we already have on hand.

1. Listing all your current resources.

It includes:
- Any previous accomplishments that you have
- Your alumni if you have any
- The different communities you are currently part of or subscribe to
- Your pre-existing network consists of close friends, vital connections, mentors, clients, acquaintances

- the social media following that you now have
- qualifications, titles, and any external credentials
- Social proof: testimonials, people we have worked with

You want to maximize the likelihood of creating opportunities by using all these elements.

2. List of People You Want To Get In Touch With

This is your list of 100 Dream people you would like to meet or get connected with. By now, you have a good understanding of the format of the list, how to structure the list.

3. List of People You Have Met But Lost Touch With

This list is equally important as you may make little of the people you previously met and forgot about or lost touch with.

These are people that you already have contact with, and it would be easier to re-establish a connection with them than reach out to new people.

In terms of scheduling time to meet with people, these individuals should be on your list of priorities.

Who do you need to become to get what you want?

Before trying to figure out what you need to do to get what you want, first pay attention to the kind of person, you need to become.

In the equation Be, Do, Have we must not get sidetracked into thinking we need to Do or Have certain things to succeed.

Most of the time, it has to do with the mindset. Attributes you positively exhibit are going to take your health, finances, spirituality, and relationships to the next level.

The question before starting any new endeavor, or continuing one should be one of: "Who do I need to be able to succeed at this?"

It's a constant effort, not a one-off push. Zig Ziglar has said, "Motivation is like milk, it expires, therefore it is important to get it daily."

What I advocate for, however, isn't motivation. It's our inner power. It's the little reminders of our inner greatness that has yet to manifest in the physical. What use is motivation when we are down with doubt, beat with exhaustion, and drained of our will?

It will get us started, but what keeps us going is the fire inside each of us. Here are some ordinary virtues that you have probably heard of but are essential for your personal growth and helping you with the Doing and Having stages.

Passion - your intrinsic drive to achieve your goal
Focus - to stay on track and cut out distractions
Grit - to keep grinding in times of struggle
Perseverance - to keep going when all seems lost
Courage - to step into the unknown and the uncertain.
Integrity - to do what is right, regardless of who is watching or not

Some virtues may be stronger than others, and you don't need to master all of them to succeed. It is just a way of placing your effort to improve certain aspects of your mindset.

Heart

If there is one virtue or attribute that you won't hear much, and that is this.

Heart.

'Heart' is difficult to conceptualize. It is a physical object, an organ, something all living humans have.

At the same time, there is a different meaning for it.

'Heart' is a combination of Grit, Perseverance, Integrity, and Courage.

I've been told many times by people much more successful than me. The reason they admire me is not because of what I've done or not done.

Heart is rare.

It is rare because not only is it a manifestation of virtues, it's also the purity of purpose and genuine intentions.

Many people other there are manipulative, lacking in moral integrity, perhaps triggered by something that has happened in their past.

Some people were hurt before, and they hate how that feels, therefore they will avoid it at all costs. They will hurt others before they let themselves get hurt. For them, it is a dog eat dog world.

They inherit ulterior motives. Their intentions are less than sincere and, at times, sinister.

People can sense this kind of behavior a mile away. Those that have encountered many people from all walks of life will pick up on it immediately.

Sometimes it isn't about how smart, sharp, or hardworking you are. Whether people choose to associate with you may very well be because you have Heart, or you don't. Having Heart doesn't mean you are the nicest person on the block, either.

It may mean that you are willing to be brutally honest to someone, even if you know it might make you look bad in the short run. You have genuine intentions of helping people. All things aside, if you have Heart, you will be able to stand out from everyone else.

Take out a sheet of paper and a pen. Write out the person you believe you need to be to do the things you need to do to achieve your goals. Now, on the top, look at your list one more time.

Realize that none of these virtues are elusive things to be obtained. They are virtues you already possess inside of you.

You are already someone who dares to step out of your comfort zone, someone who already has the tenacity, grit, and the perseverance to keep going even in hard times.

No one else holds the key except you. There is nothing outside of you that's going to empower you.

Everything you need comes from within.

Read the list over a few times if you have to and take some time to internalize this. Then it's time to move on to the next part.

Who You Need To Meet

I believe that everyone has a handful of people that come into their life that forever alters the trajectory of it.

For me, it was the mentors that I had when I first came to Hong Kong. It was also the fellow entrepreneurs that I met and worked with over the years.

It was also the digital nomads I had encountered along my journey around the world.

Without them, I wouldn't be the person I am today.

There is much to be said about particular individuals in your life. If you were lucky, you might have encountered them by chance.

If you're anything like me, however, you wouldn't leave this to chance encounter. Which means you need to find a way to meet the people that will have the most significant impact on your life.

Remember the List of 150? Chances are, your list of 150 isn't full yet, which is not a problem.

We need to create what we call the Dream 100.

I first learned about the Dream 100 while using Clickfunnels, an online sales funnel builder that helps businesses market, sell, and deliver their products online.

Clickfunnels creator Russell Brunson originally coined the idea of the Dream 100 in his book 'Expert Secrets.'

The purpose of the Dream 100 is to find potential people that could positively change your life.

I made a few changes to the original Dream 100 concept.

First off, create four categories with labels such as the list below:

- Business Owner
- Blogger
- Social Media Personality
- Celebrity

Next off, make a list of 25 people from each of these categories in a spreadsheet. Don't discriminate based on how powerful or successful they are.

Some of the names may seem daunting, but I can assure they are just as reachable as those that are less successful.

Once you have your list of 100, categorize each of the people with a new column that says Tier 1, Tier 2, or Tier 3.

Start to see where I am going with this? Remember the ladder principle? We will be using it soon. Now organize your entire list based on people in Tier 1, Tier 2, and Tier 3.

What we will be doing next is figuring out how to get in front of these quality individuals. Chances are they have a gatekeeper filtering out requests, and they will have to decide whether or not to put your request through.

If you use the right approach, they will have no problem passing you along to their boss. After all, you want them on your side.

What you want to do is infuse your outbound messages to prospects with elements of your brand, value add, and social proof.

The Path of Least Resistance vs. The Path of Frequency

It is also important to note the barrier level to reach out to a person on a particular channel. If they have a million followers on Instagram and 10,000 on Linkedin, you may be better off firing a Linkedin Message than trying to send a direct message. It's what we refer to as the *path of least resistance*.

In another case, some people prefer checking specific channels over others. We classify that as the path of frequency. For example, if they seem to check Instagram more and Linkedin rarely, it might be easier to reach out via Instagram messages.

By combining both the path of least resistance and path of frequency, you can get a good idea of what's the easiest way to get connected to an important person.

Once you do that, you want to craft and send a hyper targeted message that will get your prospects to get back to you.

Let me give you two examples of outbound messages that allowed me to secure opportunities with influential individuals.

Recently I e-mailed a US influencer by the name of Brendan Kane. My objective was to get him as a guest on my podcast. He is known for working with celebrities like Taylor Swift and Rihanna. He also was able to go from 0 to 1 million followers on Facebook and Instagram in less than 30 days.

Here is the e-mail. I started with why I was reaching out. I used my podcast as my context and platform to get a hold of Brendan.

I pitched my podcast, Live Your Edge Podcast, as an opportunity for him to share his knowledge as well as his products and services. I also mentioned other notable figures who have been on the show, which serves as social proof.

Finally, at the bottom of my message, I have a carefully crafted e-mail signature with what I do and how I add value to people. It's all about positioning yourself in a manner that allows people to help you.

Most of the time, people just put their job title. What I recommend is inserting what you DO for people or how you add value to them. One of my clients, who is a financial planner, has an e-mail signature that says, 'Helping Professionals Plan Their Next Generation's Future.'

Brendan, as well as other influencers that I've reached out to, didn't ask me how many people tuned in to my show. He didn't even ask for more information on the show itself. He just agreed. This strategy is not only limited to getting podcast interviews but also getting client meetings and other related opportunities.

Let me share another story about a meeting I had with the previous CEO of a themed park.
Before sending him an e-mail, I did my research online and looked through past interviews that he previously conducted for media outlets. I picked an exciting conversation and crafted a suitable question for him.

I quickly Googled his name and saw that he was giving a speech at an upcoming event.

I sent the e-mail with a simple greeting, mentioning the event along with the question I had in mind. I received a one-line response, "sure find me on the day let's talk."

Sure enough, I showed up to the event, and there were hundreds of people in the room. I was seated near the back and could barely see him.

After his speech, dozens of people surrounded him, handing out their name cards and asking to take pictures with him. By the time it got around to me, I had figured he would probably have forgotten about me.

All I did was say, "Hi Tom, we spoke on e-mail."

"Oh, it's you!" he replied.

We proceeded to have a fruitful discussion to the surprise of the onlookers, who had no idea how I was able to do that.

Later on, he invited me to the amusement park as a VIP, and we had a fruitful lunch discussion about work. We still keep in touch to this day, even as he is working overseas as a General Manager of another amusement park in Beijing.

I wasn't smarter than the other people in the room that wanted to connect with Tom. The only difference was that I did something that they weren't willing to do. That extra step that made all the difference.

E-mail

Is e-mail still relevant?
While many experts have advocated for moving away
from e-mail, it is still very much alive.

E-mail has been around for the last three or so
decades and will likely be relevant ten years from now.
A majority of business professionals still use e-mail, so
the chances are that you will need to use it as well.

In addition to that, e-mail provides an extra layer that
social media doesn't. You could easily send a cold
message to someone on social media, but without the
e-mail address that person, you won't be able to e-mail
them.

In recent years, spam regularly flood our inboxes. Add
that to the newsletters that we subscribe to, and it
seems impossible for some random e-mail to get our
attention.

It sounds fair to say that we would delete mail from
unfamiliar sources if the spam filter hasn't already
flagged it.

The key to getting any sort of response from a cold e-mail depends on the deliverability of your message.

The good news is that many people will avoid e-mail
because of that little barrier. They would much rather
spam everyone with a copy and paste message on
Linkedin instead. Use that to your advantage.

Most executives or essential people have assistants
taking care of their e-mail. They will promptly toss away
anything that seems like a waste of time.

The best way to break through to someone is to craft smart e-mails that get opened, read and replied to.

You could have the most clever subject line but if what you have to share isn't of substance it will quickly be thrown out. Focus your efforts on what the other person wants.

There's a channel that people tune into which is WIIFM, or 'What's it in for me.'

The moment you send something that is purely self-serving, you lose all interest. Before you can even reach out via e-mail, however, you must first find someone's e-mail.

Finding E-mail Addresses

The easiest way to find an e-mail address is through software like hunter.io. All you have to do is enter the name of the person and their domain name.

That will get you a reasonable number of valid e-mails, although you might pick up some invalid e-mails from time to time.

The way the software works is that it checks the public domain for that person's e-mail or other people in their organization for their e-mails. Then they will use that information to generate their e-mail based on the e-mail structure the system finds.

Another method includes guessing the e-mail structure of the people you are trying to reach and conduct trial and error until you get it right. This method could affect your deliverability down the road. Your domain might get flagged for spam if you send too many undelivered e-mails.

Finally, you can head over to Mechanical Turk that is run by Amazon and have outsourced workers help you uncover those e-mails.

This last method is a reasonability low cost and effective way to have other people help you figure out your list's e-mail while you focus your attention on other things.

I would wager the cost to find an e-mail these days range between 20 and 35 US cents. For a list of 100 people, that comes out to between $20 and $35.

You will need to head over to requester.mturk.com/ and create an account before proceeding.

Next off, you need to create a Task for the workers to generate results for you there.

There is a grading system for the workers that will affect the results you get. You want the accuracy of their work to be as close to 97% as possible.

The requirement levels increase so does the quality of workers that pick up your request.

You can also distinguish workers by the number of tasks they have performed. If they have completed more jobs on the platform, the chances are that the more experienced and better qualified.

There is also an option to select Master Workers, who are the top of the chain, who perform a better job but cost slightly more.

If you would like to get access to the script materials and instructions that you will need to give to the workers get them on this website: underdogmaifesto.com/mturk

Once you have the e-mails address of the people you want to reach, you have to validate them for deliverability.

Most of the time, I do not spend the time to validate e-mails because my list is very targeted, and I'll be able to figure out the right e-mail from just trial and error.

If you would like to go through the effort of verifying them, Hunter.io has a paid function that allows you to check e-mails for cents on the dollar.

The Message

The crafted message you send to each individual on your list is just as important. It will vary depending on which category they fall into.

Each message takes up a different persona, with the intent of positioning you to get a positive response.

Note that you should adopt these personas as they relate to you. It should not be used to manipulate people into connecting with you. Steer clear of doing anything that doesn't pass your ethical compass.

With that said, here are the personas or so-called "angles" you can use to reach out to different categories of hard to reach people.

The Student

When taking up the angle of a student, your objective is to learn. Therefore, the language you use in the message will be reflective of someone eager to learn something.

Here is a legend of the variables used in this sample e-mail, which has helped me secure meetings with

CEOs, and VIPs, some who have become my good friends.

{first name} = first name of the person
{channel} = where did you find out about the person through (ex: news, LinkedIn, blog post, Medium)
{topic} = topic related to their work
{organization} = can be their company or charitable organization they are part of
// = a break from the actual body of the e-mail to explain each part
{Signature} = a form of personal branding to include some of the relevant information as context for why you are reaching out. Don't just put your title and company, also use descriptions like 'Podcast Host, Entrepreneur, Speaker, etc'

Sample E-Mail
Subject: Open to learning

Hi {first name},

I found out about you through {channel} and was very impressed with the work you do for {organization}. //shows you are not randomly sending mass messages out and that you have heard of them before.

I am interested to learn more about {topic}. // shows you've done your homework and express a genuine interest to learn

Would there be a possibility of discussing more? If so, what's the best way to be in touch? // The call to action. It provides an option for them to say yes, while it is possible for them to decline.

Thanks in advance, // Signature is up to you

{Your Name}

{Signature with company name and title}

The student angle works best when you don't yet have a vast personal brand, and you don't have a company that might be able to collaborate or work with the target individual.

It's a lot easier to get through the door through this method than you might think.

The Fan

If you have been a big fan of the person you are looking to reach out to, this angle will help you get your point across as well as be inviting them to interact with you.

After all, renowned people like to talk to fans on occasion. One of the ways to structure this message is if the individual has written a book that you've read.

Legend:

{first name} = their first name

{book name} = name of the book you read from them
{action} /{result of action} = what was the step you took in your life after you read their book and what results did you achieve?
{nature of work} = what are you currently working on or doing in your profession

Sample E-mail

Subject: changed by your book

Hi {first name},

Read {book name} back in {year} and it inspired me to {action}. {result of action}

I would love to connect with you in person. I am currently {nature of work}.

Feel that there might be a match. Any thoughts on this?

Thanks in advance,

{your name}

The Fan approach can work with a broad range of categories and will easily fit all 4.

The Conference Attendee

This following e-mail template is the same one I've used over and over again to get over 57% of my target audience to respond to me. All the people I've used this template on were speakers at events or conferences.

The core purpose is to meet the speaker in person and build up a relationship with them. Going from online to offline will significantly enhance the quality of your relationship rather than staying online.

Legend:

{event/ conference} = name of event or conference
{topic 1}= first topic they are an expert in

{topic 2}= the topic you would like to discuss in more detail with them.

Sample E-mail

Subject: Your speech at {event/ conference}

Hi {first name},

I see that you will be [attending/ speaking] at {event/conference}. I would love to attend, but unfortunately, I won't be able to make it that day.

Your knowledge of {topic 1} interests me much. I would love to get your opinion on {topic 2}.

Any chance that we would be able to have a brief chat over this? If so, what's the best way to be in touch with you?

Thanks, and looking forward to hearing from you.

{your name}

Now that you are familiar with the 3 Personas you can take up when reaching out to the person on your Dream 100, what's next?

Do you send a single e-mail to them and hope for the best?

That would almost be the same as spraying and praying.

The fact is, most people send out a single message and give up when they don't receive a response.

On the one hand, that is perfectly fine; not all opportunities will materialize.

Conversely, giving up pre-maturely will limit your chances of ever finding out the answer.

I suggest following at least seven times before throwing in the towel.

Typical sales statistics will tell you that most replies come between the 5th and 12th contact point, and more give up after three tries.

Based on statistics by the SaaS company Yesware, only 8% of salespeople follow up at least five times. Those are the salespeople generating around 80% of the sales.

"70% of e-mail chains stop after just one unanswered e-mail."

It just goes to show you the value of persistence. As much as you would like to send out an e-mail and get a response the first time, you should keep the expectation that it will take several tries.

If you give up before that, you risk giving up too early.

With that said, how do you maximize the chance of getting a response back?

1. Message Content

There are a lot of factors that determine whether someone replies to you after your first approach. It might be something in your message that caught their attention. It could also be that they happen to skim those messages and forget to reply.

Perhaps your e-mail seems too generic, or spammy and they decided to give it a miss. Finally, they might have just seen the message and were too busy to get back to it.

Of course, watch out for the spam box and gatekeeper filter.

2. Cadence

Cadence has to do with how often you reach out to your target. Here is a sample cadence schedule for reaching out and following up:

Day 1 - First e-mail message
Day 3 - Follow up
Day 5 - Follow up
Day 8 - Follow up
Day 14 - Follow up
Day 21 - Follow up
Day 30 - Follow up
Day 60 - Follow up

Your cadence schedule can vary based on how aggressive you will reach out.

As you will see, channel choice plays a significant role in the cadence schedule.

3. Channel

So far, we have mentioned using e-mail to reach out. There are many different channels and mediums that you could use to complement your initial e-mail.

To get optimum results, vary your medium of outreach and the cadence of your messages.

For example, on Day 1, you might send an e-mail. On the morning of Day 2, you could call their office, leave a voicemail, and drop a message on one of their social media channels. Then on Day 3, you could send your second e-mail to follow up.

4. Value Add

Adding value is by far the best way to maximize your chances of getting a reply back.

Figure out what you could do to add value to the people you are trying to get in touch with.

You might think there may be little you could do to help someone of influence or more successful than you, but you will be mistaken.

It's never been easier to see someone's life, not in a creepy or stalking way, but to understand what matters to them.

Go on one of their online channels and look at the content they post.
1. What kind of hobbies do they have?
2. What do they enjoy doing on the weekends?
3. Do they have a family? Kids?

Use these questions as a guide for crafting a clear and concise message for adding value to people.

Struggle binds everyone

Everyone faces a struggle in their life. If their career is stable, maybe their relationships aren't. If their relationships are solid, perhaps their health isn't. There are countless examples.

Remember, no matter who you supposedly look up, they are just humans, not gods.

When we idolize people, we distance ourselves from them. We put them on a pedestal and make it difficult to connect with them.

Once you find an area of their life where they are currently facing struggles, see if you have information or connections that could help them resolve their issues.

Put that into your follow up messages. Let them know you have been keeping up with their content and that you genuinely want to help them.

Nowadays, one of the best ways to add value is to provide a platform for people to share their message.

You'll be surprised. Many people have plenty of stories to share and want to find someone to share them with.

For influencers at the top, their objective may be to spread their word to as many channels as possible.

Therefore, if you have a podcast, a YouTube channel, or any other community that could benefit the influencer, you will find that it is much easier to reach them than ever before.

No one knows how long this trend will last, but with everyone starting podcasts these days, it's going to get more and more competitive.

By just inviting people to my podcast, I was able to get above a 57% response rate from my first e-mail. It was unheard of for me. That is the power of having a platform that adds value to others.

What's Next

Alright, so now that you are reaching out to top-caliber individuals and a few of them start to respond to you, what's next?

Focus on adding value and building a relationship with them. Defer from asking anything too soon. There are a lot of takers out there. The world is full of them.

I, too, used to be one of those people. Interactions used to be 100 percent business and transactional. I realized that throughout doing that, I lost a piece of my humanity. That part of me that wants everyone to benefit, not just myself.

It all changed when one day, someone that I held in high regard did something for me that I could have never repaid.

That day I told myself that was a virtue worth aspiring to.

There's just a small population of people that genuinely give without seeking anything in return.

That is the person you might want to aspire to be. Those are the people that eventually get what they want because they have helped enough people.

I am a big fan of Zig Ziglar, an American motivational speaker, who said, "If you help enough people get what they want, ultimately they will help you get what you want."

It's one thing to ask for something, and it's another to have someone ask you if you want something.

Although the payoff won't come in the short run, it will happen in due course if you help enough people.

Chapter 19:
Building Relationships and
Asking for Favors

Meeting People at Events

Meeting people in person gives a face to the name and makes it easier for you to establish rapport.

One of the secrets that I use that most people attending events don't do is messaging and reaching out to people way in advance before the event.

Most times, people get a speaker's name card, take a picture with them, and send an e-mail post-event. As for the rest of the attendees, they probably don't receive anything in their inbox.

You could imagine a significant person is probably receiving hundreds of messages after one single event. It would be tough for one person to stand out or make a solid impression.

I've found that it is easier to connect with a VIP before an event than afterward. Similar to the example I shared about meeting the CEO by first reaching out via e-mail then relating to them on the day.

It's a very simple and straightforward strategy, but the reality is that people don't do it. Either they think they are too good for it, or believe that the chance of someone replying is slim; therefore, they don't even bother.

By doing the groundwork beforehand, you are already standing out from everyone else that just "wings" it.

Winging it works on occasion. You might have the good fortune of getting in front of someone and hit it off with them. Except you're leaving it to chance. If you want to have a systematic and sustainable way to grow your network, then you have to be professional about your approach.

Do your research. Reach out beforehand if you can. If you can't, for whatever reason, I understand entirely.

There are occasions where we don't know who exactly will turn up. Sometimes these serendipitous encounters turn out to be life-changing.

You might go into an event and come out meeting a mentor, a business partner, a key client, or a future significant other.

There have been numerous times where I stumbled into an event, without expectation, only to make life-long friends as a result.

It's silly to think everyone you meet will play a significant role in your life. You will meet people from all walks of life, and often, you may come across people will a completely different value system as you.

My metric for measuring whether to associate with someone? Don't base it on how successful they are. Measure them based on their values.

Do they align with yours?

Are they living according to values you would like to emulate?

If not, be polite and move on. It's not a popularity contest. Life is too short to be spending it with people that don't inspire you.

Be Nice Regardless

At the same time, be kind to people.

In a world that is getting smaller and smaller, be kind to everyone you encounter, else you might find yourself bitten in the ass later on.

Don't make the mistake of ignoring or giving the cold shoulder to people that don't seem as influential or smart, etc. Each person is just as important as the next.

You never know who you're speaking with and who they know. It could very well be someone unassuming that puts you in touch with an important contact.

Reputation spreads fast, so it isn't worth the short term gains. Continually asking for favors without reciprocation is a poor long term strategy.

A good rule of thumb is to give three times for each favor received.

Another thing to note is that, jobs are short. Maybe you stay in a company for 1 year, 2 years, even 10 years. Then you may eventually leave to start your own or join another firm. The idea is that careers are long. People change careers, jobs, and a person you had no real connection with five years ago is now the Chairperson of the NGO you have been trying to work with.
The person you ignored at a networking event eons ago is now commanding a team of hundreds. We often

underestimate what is possible in the span of a few years.

Building Relationships

The reality is that everyone has opportunities in front of them. Everywhere they go, all the time. The question is, *how can you capitalize on those opportunities?*

Two people can go to the same event; one leaves a handful of business cards, the other with a handful of solid relationships.

I've seen many people be the former, going around an event like a madman, continually looking for targets to hand out their name cards. It may feel good at the moment. Like you are doing something. It is our appetite for dopamine that receiving those cards that tricks us into believing that we are accomplishing something, but the truth is nothing of substance resulted from that.

We would go home, sending out a bunch of uncalibrated e-mails that go unanswered. We ask ourselves, what did we talk about again? And we realized that our conversations were shallow and lacking in depth. You don't build solid relationships on a shaky foundation.

See the interaction going deep into what motivates that person, what they care about, and what matters to them and relate this as a tree planting roots deep into the Earth.

With each of your relationships, plant your roots deep. To nurture your relationships, devote time to catch up, follow up, and touch base at least once a month or once a quarter.

Let's now assume you were able to meet or connect with someone on your Dream 100 List.

Thank People For Their Time

After you have met or spoken with them for the first time, don't forget to thank them for their time afterward.

There are many ways to do this. The fastest way is to make a video or audio recording of yourself thanking them.

If you want to add a personal touch, send over a thank you card. Be sure to confirm the mailing address either with your contact or their secretary.

Let them know that you will be sending something over and want to make sure it gets into their hands. It sounds like common sense because it is.

At the same time, what's easy to do is also easy not to do. Therefore common sense doesn't necessarily translate into everyday practice.

Adding Value

Next off, you want to look for ways to add value to them. Here are a few questions to help assist you with this.

What did you two discuss during your call, coffee, lunch?

Of the things discussed, were their interests and needs made known?

Of their needs and interests, which one is most pressing for them?

Which needs can you help them with?

Ask yourself these questions before each follow up so that you have a clear idea of how to guide the interaction forward.

Regardless, it's the thought that counts, therefore never let an opportunity to show appreciation and gratitude go to waste.

How to ask for help from influencers, CEOs, and more

Done right, this could open a vast amount of doors that would otherwise be closed to you. If done wrong, it could destroy your relationship with the person.

I remember making countless mistakes in building relationships with people.

One time I held an event bringing together several VIPs. I made a critical mistake of not explaining the expectations ahead of time. I ended up asking one of the VIPs to pay up after the event was over. He didn't take that very well.

Just imagine hearing a loud stern voice on the other side of the phone, yelling at you over the cars swishing by in the background.

After 30 seconds, our relationship was over. Let's just say I never heard from him again.
Here are a few mistakes that you make when asking for favors.

1. You are not respecting their time. People in power have less time to work with, therefore

make your request as easy to understand as possible — brief, to the point, and concise.

2. You are asking for too much. Asking too much can be a significant risk as the other person either may not have the capacity to fulfill your request or doesn't feel comfortable with fulfilling such high demand. Start with a small request. If they fill it, you could consider asking for something slightly more prominent next time. A humble request could be an introduction or a recommendation.

3. You are asking too early. If you ask too soon, you are risking putting the other person off and sending a signal to them that you are looking to get something out of them.

4. Not setting proper expectations. This is a big one. If you do not communicate the appropriate expectations, there are bound to be lots of misunderstandings that lead to fractured relationships.

The Proper Way To Ask For Favours

You're probably wondering how you could ask someone for that favor without being pushy or annoying.

1. Make the request easy to understand. Are you clear about what you want? If not, they probably won't either, and they will politely decline your request.

2. Can your request be fulfilled? How demanding is the request? If you are asking them to jump through hoops, they will also likely decline your request.

3. Ask without expectation. For example, you ask. Hi Mr. Johnson, I saw that you were close with Roy B. I've been following their work for a while, and there's an excellent opportunity to work with them coming up. Would be awesome if you could put me in touch with them. If not, that's perfectly fine and completely understand.

The last sentence is imperative because it demonstrates empathy and humility. It acknowledges that the recipient doesn't need to help you. It also shows that you don't feel entitled to their help.

Entitlement will get your requests banned before people have time to understand what it is. Quite simply, people don't like feeling like they must do something. But people love to help in ways that they can. Make them feel good about helping you.

Once you do that, they will be happy to help you again and again. So how do you give your gratitude after they have done something for you?

Some individuals only want to see you do well.

Therefore the best repay you could give them is by doing well yourself.

To do otherwise would not be of any benefit to them. To see you do well is probably one of the best forms of repaying out there because it is not something money can buy.

So to recap what we have discussed in this chapter:
-State your intentions clearly while keeping the message short, concise, and relevant.
-Add value instead of trying to impress people.

-Make incremental asks and focus on getting a reply back.
-Remember to thank people.

Calibration and Cooperation

What is calibration?

The Oxford definition describes calibration as the act of determining the graduations of something.

A simple example is the markings of a scale, where you would zero the range to avoid creating reading errors.

In a social situation, calibration is about understanding where you stand in relation to another person.

If you assert that the person you are with is friendly, open, and trustworthy, chances are you will be more likely to disclose personal information about yourself.

Being vulnerable with this person is not necessarily a default, but it is somewhat easier to accomplish.

In another situation, you encounter someone that presents themselves to you with a sense of skepticism. You probably won't share much personal information with this person.

For cooperation to happen, both parties must be open to working together. Being the ability to calibrate based on each situation will serve you well when it comes to picking who you want to work with, and who you want to steer clear of.

Chapter 20:
Rewriting Your Destiny

Who do you aspire to?

Who do you really aspire to model after?

This is a very important and profound question that we must ask at one point or another.

We should deeply question our role models and heroes, people whose success we want to emulate.

We should be careful who our heroes are. The same way you don't want to learn from someone that hasn't done what you want to do, you don't want to learn from people whose values you don't want to exhibit.

Just because someone has material success doesn't make them the best example of being. Let your life flow through your values.

Who aspires to you?

Who are those people that aspire to be like you?

Have you made an effort to connect with them?

To listen to them, to learn from them. I genuinely believe we have something to learn from everyone.

To have someone aspire to you, it means someone sees something about you that is virtuous.

Sometimes we are aware of this virtue. Often we are blinded to it. We take it for a given, something that comes naturally to us.

To people that admire you might ask, "What is it about me that inspires you? Empowers you?"

You may be surprised by the answer you get. That is because the values we strive for are very likely the values we already have.

Let's take courage, for instance.

Courage isn't something you get from the store. It exists in the same space as fear.

They come in the same package.

If you can feel fear, you also have within yourself the power to feel courage.

Courage, therefore, is a conscious decision to act in spite of fear.

To someone less aware of themselves, they would be stuck in the fear dynamic, always in search of something that would give them courage.
Little do they realize that courage has always been a part of them.

It's their choice whether to truly see their strength the same way they see their weakness.

When you lose sight of your virtue, allow others to remind you.

It's not as a form of validation but as a form of help.

If you can let your ego down, you will be able to glimpse into your greatest virtues. If you guard it tightly, it will elude you and take you further away from what you seek.

You'll be spinning your wheels, going nowhere fast.

Caring is Underrated

Nowadays, society seems like a place where not caring is the modus operandi, and caring appears like a weakness. It looks a lot cooler not to care, to shrug things off.

As a result, we become cold toward others.

At the end of the day, how would you like to be remembered?

It's easy to quantify success as a kind of lifestyle you can afford for yourself and your family — the kind of achievements and accolades that come with that kind of material success.

At the same, that's not the only kind of success you could have.

You could also be someone that genuinely gave a shit about those you came across. It wasn't about trying to get something out of them.

One of my mentors told me over and over.

'People are bound to use you for good or for ill. If no one can find a way to use you, then you aren't of value to anyone.'

It sounds terrible at first blush, but I can assure you it's not.

The reality is that as you get higher and higher up on the totem pole or 'ladder of material success,' people are going to want to get a part of it for their gain.

Allow them.

There's no use trying to resist or defend against it. You'll waste precious energy fighting it.

Instead, use that effort to do more for others even if they use it for their gain. Of course, if you realize they are doing that, you don't need to cater to them deliberately.

Just allow what happens. If they want to leverage your name, let it as long as it doesn't mess with your reputation.

Once you surrender to this idea, you will no longer be playing the game of life in defense. Playing defense is where you are always guarding yourself against the outside world.

It's no sane way to live.

There are many well-known change-makers like Tony Robbins, with thousands of people using the pictures they take with him at an event to promote their agenda.

There's no harm in allowing it to happen, for all you know that could have been of great use for them, and it allowed them to open more doors.

Perhaps they may help you in the future. Maybe they won't.

It doesn't matter either way.

What matters is that you showed your care. You indicated that you are willing to give. When we start giving more, we open ourselves to receiving.

There is no chance of receiving when you are looking only to take.

When we continuously look for new ways to give, we don't stop to keep count of what we have done for others.

Sometimes we forget, and that's fine.

When you do something good for someone, forget it. When someone does something good for you, *remember it.*

That will provide you with the sanity to keep giving, over and over, even when people don't give back.

It's not a scoreboard where a number says you've made it.

The 'strongest indicator' is someone coming back to you one day and saying, 'You know what, what you did for me all those years ago made the biggest difference for me.'

It is moments like that, which will remind you what matters in the grand scheme of things.

That you left the world better than you came into it.

At least that is what my journey has taught me. If all of us could help one more or two more people each day, instead of looking to get benefits, imagine how far that would cascade.

Give care to another thought and commit to being more caring to the people in your life.

'People don't remember you for what you did, but how you made them feel.'

So make them remember that you have cared, for there is probably no better way to be remembered.

The Curse of Privilege

Privilege is for a handful of people who were either born with certain societal rights or were given them down the road. There are those with an inherited advantage over you.

They may have gone to the best schools. Their parents might have had the right connections.

Some look at privilege with a sense of resentment.

"Those people were born with a silver spoon; therefore, it is normal for them to get those kinds of opportunities."

Or

"Yeah, if I had the kind of resources that she has, I would be so much more successful."

The problem with resentment and envy is that it serves no one. The person you are critiquing doesn't gain or lose anything, and you certainly don't learn anything.

If anything, people that do that provide themselves with an out — a way not to strive for their greatness.

They justify where they are in life based on what other people are doing.

It would be far simpler to blame it on something external to yourself than have to face definite struggle and the uncertainty of ever seeing success.

Here's a truth bomb. You don't know what is going on in their life.
Having known and befriended many wealthy people in my life, I got a chance to get under the pretense.

People from privilege have different problems.
Problems that we probably don't have growing up poor or in the middle class.

I have a friend that struggles with what they want to do with their life. He has everything that he could ever want, yet has no idea how to find meaning with what he has.

There is a constant struggle to step outside the shadow of someone successful in their family. Comparisons between siblings, relatives were frequent.

After all, there was an expectation that if you have much, you should be able to do more with it.

Someone that didn't have that baggage wouldn't have those expectations. After all, if they are at the bottom, there's nothing to expect. They could only go up from there.

It doesn't matter what other people have. The question is, 'how do I level the playing field?'

The answer to that, by now, you will know it as improving in the arts of creating leverage.

You are creating leverage through your skillset, your network, and your community.

Leverage is the great equalizer.

Finding Abundance

The feeling of abundance was something that was simply out of this world for me. Coming from an environment and thinking of scarcity, it was easy to accept mediocrity.

To one that lives in scarcity, nothing will ever be enough. For someone that embraces abundance, there is enough for everyone to go around.

I could have accepted my circumstances, followed the rules, and just lived how others wanted me to live.

Instead of being held down by setbacks, I used each of those setbacks as stepping blocks forward.

Even as the future is mostly uncertain, there is a beauty to it. It is because of the uncertainty that we are allowed to thrive.

After all, there is no glory if everyone had absolute certainty all the time.

It depends on whether we choose to dwell on the struggle or shift our focus towards what is possible.

We step out of the darkness of our doubts and into the light. The light which permeates every corner of our journey with hope and revelation.

When we choose to look at everything around us with wonder and possibility, we will start to see how many opportunities are indeed around us.

It's just whether we are willing to grasp them.

The Phoenix Within

I liken the evolution of that of an underdog to top dog as a phoenix, rising from the ashes.

You too can be that phoenix — no matter where you grew up or where you started in life matters not. What matters is the kind of person you become as a result.

The struggles and trials you've endured have set you up on this path, at this moment in time. They have shaped and hardened your resolve, but don't let it harden your heart.

Let your past, in hindsight, sharpen your foresight into the future.

I hope that one day our paths do cross, and you will have many great stories to share with me, as I have with you.

Until then, whether sooner or later, I'll see you on the other side.

Acknowledgements

I wouldn't have imagined that one day I would become an author. If I had to do it all by myself, this book probably wouldn't be able to materialize.

It was through the guidance of my mentors, friends, and loved ones that all of this was made possible.

Thanks, mom and dad for your unwavering love and patience with me. It looks like I turned out alright.

Thank you, Sophia, for your constant love, support, and encouragement in my journey.

Special thanks to Brandon Leuangpaseuth for providing many thought-provoking ideas to improve the manuscript and helping with the editing. Thanks for going above and beyond for this project. You're the man!

Thank you, Mr. Po Chung, Eric, and Roger, for your wisdom and mentorship.

Dicky, Nolan, Jack, and Tony, thank you for believing in me. Your friendship means the world to me.

Thanks to Danny and Vincent for our epic adventures together during my nomadic adventures in the last two years.